THE SYSTEMIC ANALYSIS OF JUDAISM

Program in Judaic Studies
Brown University
BROWN JUDAIC STUDIES
Edited by
Jacob Neusner,
Wendell S. Dietrich, William Scott Green, Ernest S. Frerichs,
Calvin Goldscheider, Alan Zuckerman

Project Editors (Project)

David Blumenthal, Emory University (Approaches to Medieval Judaism)
William Brinner (Studies in Judaism and Islam)
Ernest S. Frerichs, Brown University (Dissertations and Monographs)
Lenn Evan Goodman, University of Hawaii (Studies in Medieval Judaism)
William Scott Green, University of Rochester (Approaches to Ancient Judaism)
Norbert Samuelson, Temple University (Jewish Philosophy)
Jonathan Z. Smith, University of Chicago (Studia Philonica)

Number 137
THE SYSTEMIC ANALYSIS OF JUDAISM

by
Jacob Neusner

THE SYSTEMIC ANALYSIS OF JUDAISM

by
Jacob Neusner

Scholars Press
Atlanta, Georgia

THE SYSTEMIC ANALYSIS OF JUDAISM

Library of Congress Cataloging-in-Publication Data

Neusner, Jacob, 1932-
  The systemic analysis of Judaism.

  (Brown Judaic studies ; no. 137)
  Includes index.
  1. Judaism--Study and teaching. 2. Religion--
Study and teaching. I. Title. II. Series.
BM71.N47 1988 296'.07   87-32401
ISBN 1-55540-204-6 (alk. paper)

Printed in the United States of America
on acid-free paper

In memory of

Alexander Singer

1962-1987

who died in the fullness of life
for the cause to which in full intent he had chosen to devote his life.

He made the ascent to live his life
in the State of Israel.
He gave his life in the defense of the State of Israel,
and the entire People of Israel everywhere
recognize his gift of life in their service and mourn his death.

Rare and privileged is the one
who walks a single, straight path
in the ascent from life to death.

Many join
his parents and family in mourning this grievous loss,
even without having known him.

For we know what he stood for,
and honor and cherish his ideal,
because he gave his life for it.

CONTENTS

Preface

The academic study of religion, which, in its present form, began after World War II, has reached the end of the first phase in its renaissance in the USA and Canada. Distinguishing the study of religion from the study of theology marked a break with a long and honorable past; in Western Europe, South Africa, and to some measure also in New Zealand and Australia, the study of religion then and now finds its academic sponsorship in theology or divinity faculties, and not in the liberal arts. And in the worlds of Islam and Buddhism, religions are practiced, and the practice of a religion involves mastery of its holy books. But religion is not studied. We deal therefore with a particularly Western, and distinctively American and Canadian, phenomenon, with connections, to be sure, in Western Europe – an American invention within the academy, and, I think, one that is typically American at that.

A development in the humanities with no interesting parallel overseas, except for some isolated figures in other parts of the English-speaking world, the new field proposes to undertake what we call "the religious study of religion." That phrase, a slogan of the field, means to exclude the theological study of religions in the name of a given religion, for example, the judgment, whether descriptive or analytical, of a given theological system upon the nature of religion. It further means to set aside the sociological or psychological study of religion, the study of religious institutions or personalities within the study of history, and similar, entirely appropriate, but essentially tangential approaches. The premise of the academic study of religion is that we can study not only religions but religion, and, while not new, that conviction in our own circumstance represents a quite fresh attitude toward what we do when we study something we classify as religion.

The truth is that, at the present time, we can scarcely point to substantial evidence that the academic study of religion, as distinct from theological studies, mostly by believers, of the religions they believe, whether academic or theological in institutional sponsorship, goes forward at all. The reason is that the evidences of an academic field with its own program of inquiry, its own mode of framing and answering questions, its own well-considered manner of developing useful hypotheses and testing them – these commonplaces of academic learning are difficult to locate. Clearly, studies of religions flourish, both under the auspices of church, synagogue, mosque, and the like, and also in universities. Journals print learned articles about this and that in Buddhism,

Judaism, Christianity, Islam, and on and on, and authors and editors and sponsors of the journals therefore appear to take for granted people will read the journals. But just as, in the Journal of the American Oriental Society, it is assumed that a few people will read this, and a few others, that, but no one will read everything from Sumerian to modern Japanese, with the whole "Orient" – Turkey to the Aleutians – thrown in hither and yon, so it is taken for granted by editors of such disparate journals as *Numen, Harvard Theological Review,* and *History of Religion,* that no one is likely to read everything in any given issue. There is no predicting the order of articles, no explaining their layout, no accounting for what is included and what rejected. Indeed, given the self-referential tone and reverent self-absorption of the authors, one might have reason to wonder whether anyone is expected to read anything in those and similar journals.

True, the generality of academic journals seldom provides a stage for dancing prose. But the problem is not merely that, in the academic world, people in graduate education rarely are taught to write articles (let alone books), since most of their teachers do not write articles and have published, if any books at all, at most, their own dissertations,. But the reason is entirely intellectual. It is that no common program draws together data from different species of the genus, religion, into a study of the genus and not only the species. The author of an article on a topic in Buddhism writes for specialists on Buddhism. But then that author is in the field of Buddhology, I suppose, or philology or text-study or whatever. The author of an article on an Islamic subject along these same lines assumes that the readers know why the subject matters and how other scholars will make use of the findings at hand. The absence of a common address to an academic field, religion, proves striking even when we merely survey the topics of articles in the journals, but turns into an urgent (if not entirely humorless) question when we ask why the editors put this beside that, or this in front of that. In fact, there is no order, because there is no program. A journal in which none can explain the sequence and order of the articles testifies that there is none in the field that the articles supposedly comprise. And that testimony seems to me probative.

What is wrong is not that there is no field, religion, but only, religions. It is that the people who claim to undertake to study religion study only religions. They scarcely pretend to be interested in religion, for instance, in drawing conclusions, from the data they have mastered, about the nature or the possibilities of religion in general. It is then the absence not of generalization but of hypotheses transcending the case at hand that marks the intellectual vacuity of studies of religions, as against the study of religion. In fact, in the social sciences people do frame hypotheses about religion and they do test them, they do follow a program of sustained inquiry into issues of theory, tested against the evidence of concrete fact, and, above all, they do find it possible to follow research in some topic other than the one on which a given scholar himself or herself is working. Competent scholars do not study the sociology of Judaism in Afula or of the Latter Day Saints in Peru in isolation from other religious sociology, but the sociology of religion. They want to know about how we may learn about the psychology of religious people or communities from the data of a particular community or person. And this is the case for the other social sciences. That means they resort, at all stages of analysis and interpretation of data, to issues of comparison and contrast. Consequently, the names that prove paramount in the academic study of religion derive from sociology, economics, psychology, for instance, Durkheim and Weber, Marx and (again) Weber and Sombart, Freud and Jung, and the like. Nor are all the paramount intellects figures of the later nineteenth and earlier twentieth centuries. In our own part of the twentieth century, anthropologists have taught more about the study of religions than, in their study of religion, they can have imagined they would teach. In this context the names of Geertz, Douglas, Leach, and many others, come to mind. And the intellectual gifts of sociologists and psychologists and historians continue to enrich the study of religion, not only religions.

But the social sciences in the nature of things do their work best when they concentrate on the hard data of contemporary observation. The economist, lacking accurate facts, can scarcely know what to make of the economy of the ancient world, and a sociology of ancient Israel commonly invokes theological, not secular, categories at every step of the way. Colleagues who claim to describe "the social world" of Paul begin in categories that no working sociologist could use in any other context but the handful of letters attributed to Paul. The reason for the present impasse is that social scientists require data that most religious traditions find it difficult to prove. For when we study a religious tradition, it is ordinarily through its literature and art and other enduring testimonies, and these, in the nature of things, demand that concern for particularity and specificity that we identify with the humanities, not with the social sciences. The upshot is very simple. The academic study of religion aims at generalization. But the people who carry on that study work on materials that make generalization exceedingly difficult. The social sciences, which have as their task the framing and testing of generalizations, by contrast, provide for the study of religions an asymmetrical model, the theory not entirely serving the kind of facts available for the framing and testing of the theory. In Chapter One I explain how I propose to do things right.

In this book I carry forward and spell out my conception of the way forward for the academic study of religion. It is to undertake what I call "the systemic analysis of religion," a concept I define in Chapters One and Two and then attempt to illustrate and exemplify in the following chapters. Part One provides two theoretical statements and an example of the implications of the analytical study of a religious system for one possible reading of the Pentateuch. Part Two addresses the reading of religion as a chapter in political economy. Part Three compares two religious systems. The work then follows my prescription of description, analysis, and interpretation. Part Two goes over results of my *The Economics of Judaism. The Initial Statement,* and Parts One and Three do the same for bits and pieces of my *The Bavli and its Sources, The Making of the Mind of Judaism,* and *The Formation of the Jewish Intellect: Making Connections and Drawing Conclusions in the Traditional System of Judaism.* Nothing in this book repeats ideas already set forth in my *First Principles of Systemic Analysis,* which follows a quite different program in general and in detail.

My conviction for thirty years is that what I learn about Judaism may serve to clarify the nature of religion, not only of Judaism (or of the Jews). That conviction derives from my deeper faith – it is hardly a demonstrable fact of history and society – that the Jews and Judaism form an interesting and exemplary mode of humanity. On the one side, they are not unique, but they also are sufficiently unlike to prove interesting. Like others they prove susceptible of comprehension and reasoned explanation. Unlike others, they present interesting possibilities, a new set – in the language of Jonathan Z. Smith – of *e.g.*'s, for analysis. I should hold that, in its own setting and context, the same is to be said for Christianity, and if and when the academic study of religion ever reaches and shapes the study of other important and exemplary religious systems of the world, Islam, for instance, I am sure that colleagues will come to the same conclusion. As I point out in Part III, Judaism claims to be "unique," and Christianity to be "absolute," and both claims, theologically necessary and correct, testify to what it means to be not Judaic or Christian but religious. Then the academic intellect too makes its judgment and sets forth its claim: there really is religion, not only religions. Now to prove it, not merely to believe it – that is a task for the twenty-first century.

And, coming to the end of a century and reaching now well into the final third of my own career, I may be forgiven for a certain urgency about the matter. For I should propose that, if we cannot prove that commonality of humanity, religion, really exists, and not only religions, and if – to continue the negative formulation, we do not make it possible for different people talking about different things to different people nonetheless to attain a shared understanding of the one social world that all of them comprise, then there will not be a twenty-second century, or even much of a twenty-first one worth having. So it seems to me, then, that the stakes in the academic study of religion are not negligible.

Jacob Neusner

Erev Sukkot 5748
October 8, 1987

Program in Judaic Studies
Brown University
Providence, Rhode Island 02912-1826

Prologue

Which Judaism?

A religious system that appeals to the Hebrew Scriptures or Old Testament in setting forth a world view and describing a way of life addressed to a particular "Israel" comprises a Judaism. While every Judaism known in history has appealed to the Old Testament, any definition of a single normative Judaism requires theological judgments that rest upon conviction. Description, rather than conviction, begins in the recognition of the variety of Judaic systems known not only in today's world, but also in the past. For diverse Judaisms have flourished over time, from the completion of the Pentateuch, the five books of Moses, in ca. 500 B.C., to our own day. All of them have identified "Israel," meaning God's holy people, and all have appealed to passages of Scripture, particularly the Pentateuch, for justification for the respective systems that they have set forth. The symbolic system of each Judaism, however, rests upon a system particular to itself. One Judaism may appeal for its generative symbol to "the Torah," meaning not only the Five Books of Moses but a much larger heritage of divine revelation in the media of both writing and oral formulation and transmission. Another Judaism may identify as its principal mode of expression a way of life centered upon cultic holiness realized within the community, as with the Essenes in general, and the Qumran Essenes in particular. The symbol of that Judaism will be not the Torah but the table at which everyday food was consumed in a state of cultic cleanness. A third Judaism, Orthodoxy of the Zionist sort, in our own time, may utilize the Messiah-theme and identify the formation of a Jewish state with the beginning of the attainment of the Messianic age.

These and other examples of Judaisms point both to the diversity of the religious systems that identify themselves as "Judaism" but also to commonalities among them. These are, first, appeal to Scripture (but each to its own florilegium of verses as prooftexts for preselected propositions); second, address to "Israel" (but each with its own identification of its devotees with "Israel" or, at least, "the true Israel"); and, third, a program of concrete actions in the workaday world for the realization of the faith (but every Judaism has its own notion of the essential or required actions). The theological definition of Judaism yields only diversity, therefore, and a comparison of ideas about God or the definition of the Torah held among several Judaisms would yield equivalent diversity (just as comparisons among Christianities' Christologies or ecclesiologies presents considerable points of disagreement). Defining all Judaisms within a single structure, rather than through a search for common points of theology, by contrast, produces a clear picture of shared and fundamental traits.

When we state in general terms the pentateuchal story, which is shared among all Judaisms, we find ourselves retelling in the setting of mythical ancestors the experience of exile and return, alienation and redemption, that actually characterized the Jews' history from the destruction of the temple of Jerusalem in 586 B.C. to the return to Jerusalem (Zion) and the rebuidling of the temple about a century and a half later. While not all Jews were sent by the conquerers, the Babylonians, into exile in 586, and among those who did go away, still fewer came back from 540 onward, when the new masters of the Middle East, the Iranians under Cyrus of the Persian dynasty, the compilers of the Pentateuch treated as normative the experience of being sent away from the land and returning to the land, hence, exile and redemption. Thus Abraham was commanded to leave Ur of the Chaldees, in the general vicinity of the Babylonia to which the exiles had been sent, and to wander to the land. His "children" (within the theory of "Israel" as one big family) gained the land but lost it to Egypt; then they underwent wanderings in the desert until they regained the land. The land was held not permanently and as a settled fact of life but only on condition of obeying God's Torah, meaning, revelation, including law for the conduct of everyday life, and so living up to the covenant made by God with successive progenitors of "Israel." This pentateuchal story set forth the stipulative quality of possession of the land and treated the life of the people, Israel, as subject to qualifications and conditions, not as a given. Setting forth both the conditionality of Israel's existence but also the promise of reward for obedience to God's covenant, the Pentateuch laid out a fundamental structure which, thereafter, defined the generative experience of all Judaisms. Each would both set forth an account of its "Israel" that treated the given as subject to conditions, but also defined those conditions that would provide security and resolve doubt. A Judaism, in general, therefore both provoked resentment and doubt, but also resolved the doubt and provided remission for resentment, and that fundamental structural pattern, expressed as (in political and this-worldly terms) exile and redemption, characterizes every known Judaism.

But among Judaisms, a single one predominated from late antiquity to modern times and remains a powerful influence among Jews even today. That Judaism is the one under discussion in this book. It is the Judaism that finds its definitive statement in the myth that, when Moses received the Torah, revelation, from God at Mount Sinai, God gave the Torah through two media, writing and also memory. The Written Torah of this Judaism of the dual Torah is represented by Scripture or the Old Testament. The other Torah, formulated orally and transmitted only in memory, was handed on for many generations, from Moses down to the great sages of the early centuries of the Common Era (C.E.=A.D.), when it finally reached writing in documents produced by sages, who bore the honorific title, "rabbi," "my lord." This kind of Judaism bears several titles, one, rabbinic, because of the character of its leadership, another, Talmudic, because of its principal document, and, for theological reasons, "classical" or "normative," as indeed became the fact from the promulgation of the Talmud onward. Talmudic Judaism may best be traced through the unfolding of its writings, therefore, because it was in writing, in study in academies, through the teaching of holy men (in contemporary times, women as well) qualified for saintliness by learning, specifically, mastery of the Torah through discipleship, that that Judaism took shape. Just as one may write the history of Roman Catholic Christianity by tracing the story of the papacy, though that history would not be complete, and the history of Protestant Christianity through telling the story of the Bible in the world since the Reformation, so the history of the Judaism of the dual Torah takes shape in the tale of its holy books.

Among these, the first to reach closure was the Mishnah, an account, in the form of a law-code, of the holy life of "Israel," in the household and in the temple, in the family and in the village, to be compared to Plato's *Republic* and Aristotle's *Politics* as a picture of an ideal polity. The Mishnah came to conclusion in ca. A.D. 200, after about a century of sustained composition among successive generations of sages. While some of its materials go back into the first centuries, and basic facts even to scriptural times, the fundamental statement of the document as a whole is worked out as a complete and self-contained system, a cogent philosophy, not as the result of a sedimentary process of tradition. The emphasis of the Mishnah's philosophy stresses stability, order, the self-contained and stationary character of society, position, wealth and resources, all things in their proper place and under their proper name, reminiscent of the priestly account of creation in Genesis 1:1-2:4. Since, in the preceding century, with the destruction of the second temple in A.D. 70, the defeat of a major rebellion against Rome, then at the height of its power, in A.D. 132-135, and the disruption of the life of the Jews in their land ("Israel" in the "land of Israel," in theological terms), the people had known chaos, the document described the opposite of the everyday reality. Obedience to its design for the life of its "Israel" then promised what its authorship deemed critical.

If the Mishnah came forth as a utopian design in response to an existential crisis, however, it soon was turned into something quite different, namely, the constitution, along with Scripture, for the life of the Jews wherever they lived, not only in the Land of Israel but also in Babylonia, and for the here and now, not only for the time, envisaged by the Mishnah's authorship and therefore subjected to ample legislation, when the temple would be rebuilt. For the Mishnah was adopted as the basic law code of administration and government by the Jewish ethnarch of Palestine, which is to say, the patriarch of Israel in the

Land of Israel, and many of the sages of the Mishnah's schools were employed as his clerks and administrators. Consequently a document only partially addressing the everyday life, in its divisions devoted to family affairs and civil law, but largely focused upon the temple and its cult, in its divisions concerning the conduct of the cult in everyday circumstances (the fifth division, Holy Things), on festivals (the second division, Appointed Times), and in regard to cultic cleanness (the sixth division, Purities), was reformed. The exegesis of the Mishnah now focused upon only part of its contents. The systemic study and application of those parts of the contents of the Mishnah pertinent to the everyday life of Israel in the Land of Israel in ca. A. D. 400 yielded a systematic restatement, known as the Talmud of the Land of Israel ("Yerushalmi"), and, in ca. A.D. 600, the counterpart for the Jews in Babylonia was the Talmud of Babylonia ("Bavli"). Of these two Talmuds, the latter, became paramount and authoritative and through its sustained exegesis and application under nearly all circumstances and in every age defined the Judaism of the dual Torah, that is to say, Judaism, from its time to our own. For even today all Judaisms, Reform, Orthodox, Conservative, Reconstructionist, appeal to the Bavli and related writings as the foundation-document for all else, while, of course, differing on points of interpretation and even the weight and authority of that writing and the other documents that appeal to it.

The Judaism of the dual Torah, appealing as it did to Scripture as much as to the Mishnah, in the time following the closure of the Mishnah took up certain books of Scripture and read them in light of its larger systemic interests. That reading yielded two classifications of scriptural exegesis, called, in Hebrew, Midrash. The first involved the rereading of legal passages of the books of Exodus, Leviticus, Numbers, and Deuteronomy, with an eye to discovering the connections, especially the harmonies, between the laws of the Mishnah and the statements of Scripture. The point is repeatedly made that the rules of the Mishnah are not autonomous, resting only upon reason, but depend upon their origin in divine revelation in written form, that is, Scripture. Sifra, to Leviticus, Sifré, to Numbers, and another Sifré, to Deuteronomy, repeatedly make that single point. Mekhilta, to Exodus, stands apart from these documents but in its program and polemic is coherent with them. The second classification of scriptural exegesis encompasses compilations of scriptural exegeses that concern historical and social laws, as distinct from the everyday rules for the workaday world that the Mishnah sets forth. These documents of scriptural exegesis provide a theology for Israel's life in history and beyond, identifying those social rules and historical points of regularity that will guide Israel through time. They cover Genesis, in Genesis Rabbah, Leviticus, in Leviticus Rabbah, and other writings as well. Yet other compilations of scriptural exegeses cover the synagogue liturgy, particularly the lections for special occasions, and deliver messages on the same themes. In these ways the writings of the Oral Torah, in relationship to the Written Torah, form that "one whole Torah of Moses, our lord," that sets forth the definitive and exhaustive statement of Judaism.

That Judaism of the dual Torah from the seventh century onward flourished within Christendom and Islam. Its success in both worlds derived from its capacity to explain, for the Jews, the condition of the Israel that they unanimously concurred they constituted. The dual Torah explained the present and accounted for a worthwhile future. In the context of Christianity it addressed the Christian *défi* of Israel, with its claim that the Messiah had already come and "Israel after the flesh" had had its redemption when the second temple was built; that "Israel" was now another Israel, after the spirit; that history focused not upon holy Israel but upon Jesus Christ. The answer of the dual Torah, from its documents in the fourth century (the Yerushalmi) onward, was that the Messiah would come when Israel obeyed the Torah; that Israel after the flesh was the true and only family of Abraham, Isaac, and Jacob; and that what happened in all of history responded to the moral condition of Israel and God's judgment of Israel. Islam, later on, posed a less acute, because less specific, challenge, since it did not claim to supersede, but only to succeed and form the seal of, the revelation of God to Moses (and Jesus). The subordination of Israel to Islam found ample explanation in the apologia already composed in response to the triumph of Christianity in the time of Constantine, in the fourth century. That is why the Judaism of the dual Torah prevailed from Morocco to India, from France to Hungary and Romania, Lithuania, Poland, and the Ukraine, and from Algeria to England, in medieval times, and throughout the places in the Western hemisphere, Africa, and in Australasia, to which Jews migrated in the nineteenth and twentieth centuries. In Europe and North America producing variations and varieties in the forms of Reform Judaism, Orthodoxy, Conservative Judaism, and the like, that single Judaism, appealing to its well-defined canon of writings, absorbing within itself an extraordinarily varied range of spiritual impulses, mystical and philosophical alike, predominated, and, so far as Jews seek to work out a religious system for the explanation of their existence as a social group, defines Judaism today. Evidence for that fact derives from the character of heresies in medieval and modern times. In every instance, the heresy denied a principle critical to the Judaism of the dual Torah, or affirmed a belief denied by it. An example of the former is Karaism, from the ninth century, which denied the belief that there was an oral, as well as a written, Torah revealed at Sinai, and of the latter, Sabbateanism, in the seventeenth and eighteenth centuries, which affirmed that the Messiah had come and was not an observer of the laws of the Torah at all. The first important Judaic system to stand wholly outside of the symbolic system and mythic structure of the Judaism of the dual Torah is the Judaism of Holocaust and Redemption, which has taken shape since 1967, and the influence of which is presently considerable; but no one now knows the future history of that Judaism. Now to the explanation of what I mean by "systemic analysis of religion," for the case of a Judaism.

Part I

SYSTEMIC ANALYSIS OF A RELIGION

THE CASE OF A JUDAISM

Chapter One

Defining the Systemic Study of Judaism

When the academic study of religion works well, it forms a union of the strength of the social sciences and the power of the humanities. When it works poorly, it offers vacuous generalizations, beyond all testing (if not, indeed, surpassing all comprehension) based on a skewed or even awry sample of evidence, the probative character of which no one even can assess. There is no easy way of securing the benefits of both social science and humanistic learning for the academic study of religion, standing as it does on the margins between sociology and philology, economics and text-study, history and philosophy. Requiring the gifts of two quite distinct, if intersecting, realms of learning, the academic study of religion has yet to frame its demands to each. In order to address this problem I have been trying to form a theory of how to study a religion in accord with a program of generalization serving religion in general, that is to say, to study one religion as I might any other religion.

It seems to me the simplest fact of all religions, hence of religion, is that religion is something people do together, something they do to accomplish shared goals. Hence religion is a social fact, and the artifacts of religion, texts, drawings, dances, music, for example, form components of a shared, therefore social, system. Religion encompasses a shared world view, explains a shared way of life, identifies the social entity of those that realize the one and live by the other; it forms the integrating power that makes a single statement out of politics and economics, as much as out of the individual's life cycle and the communal calendar that distinguishes one season from another and marks a day as holy. In order to study such a protean and encompassing, definitive element of the social system, I need to be able to describe it, and, to do that, I have to know what data will serve my inquiry. To answer that question, I ask three simple questions: what is the world view of a religion? what is the way of life of a religion? And what is the social entity to which the world view is addressed and which realizes or embodies the way of life? The answers to these questions in hand, I can describe a religious system.

In analyzing that system – and this draws me toward the work of comparison and contrast – I have a further intellectual labor. It is to find a way of holding together the three components of a religious system. What serves is a hypothesis that reads these components as elements of an answer to a question.

If I can propose a single encompassing statement that constitutes the system's recurrent message and judgment, then I can claim to know the answer. From that knowledge, I can make a good guess at the question to which the answer responds. And then I can test my proposed hypotheses through the evidence at hand. Once I have come to a theory on the description of the system – ethos, ethics, social entity – and the analysis of that system – urgent question, compelling answer – I reach the stage of interpretation, at which, of course, the comparison of system to system forms the elementary stage in the study of the systems of the religious life. That, sum and substance, seems to me a theory of the academic study of religion that derives strength from both the humanities' powers of a close reading of a single and particular document and the culture that produced that document, and also the social sciences' powers of theoretical explanation of the whole. I should find in the humanities the account of the species, in the social sciences, the theory of the genus. In all, therefore, I see the academic study of religion, in its present nascent age, in the model of natural history in its earlier phases, in the eighteenth and nineteenth centuries, before Darwin. And I should claim that in what I call the systemic study of religion, in my case, Judaism, we do study not only religions, but – in goal, therefore also in detail – religion.

Let me proceed to my own work, for example. The particular problem that has occupied my attention for nearly thirty years and about two hundred volumes – scholarly books, monographs, translations, academic textbooks, exercises in *haute vulgarisation,* and the like – is to work out how in the study of religion we move from literary evidence to a theory about the nature of the religious world that produced the evidence in hand, and thence to hypotheses of general intelligibility about religion. I summarize this process as a move from [1] text, to [2] context, to [3] matrix. It is that first step, text to context, that has occupied me for three decades. In essays such as those collected in this book, which summarize results published in sustained monographs elsewhere, I share some of what I have learned. All of us who study particular religions have to work our way from the particular thing we know to the things we think we are learning, and I want to place on display here how I have tried to do so.

My own work then is meant to exemplify possible ways of the study of a religious system. It always concerns exemplary classics of Judaism and how they form a cogent statement. These classical writings, produced from the first to the seventh centuries A.D., form the canon of a particular statement of Judaism, the Judaism of the dual Torah, oral and written. That canon defined Judaism in both Christendom and Islam from the seventh century to the present. The circumstances of its formation, in the beginnings A.D. Western civilization, the issues important to its framers, the kind of writings they produced, the modes of mediating change and responding to crisis – these form the center of interest. That is why in the sequence of my major projects I lay out first the classical religious literature on which I work and also those lessons out of the methods and results of my own work that may serve for purposes of generalization. In this way I have tried to make my work serve as a useful model, a source of *examplia gratia,* both method and substance, for colleagues. Why the stress on these particular writings? The reason is simple. They speak for what Brian Stock has called a "textual community." The classic documents of the Judaism that took shape in the first through sixth centuries A.D. and that has predominated since then, the Judaism of the dual Torah, represent the collective statement and consensus of authorships (none is credibly assigned to a single author and all are preserved because they are deemed canonical and authoritative) and show us how those authorships proposed to make a statement to their situation – and, I argue, upon the human condition. What I do with these writings, as is clear from what has already been said, is in three stages.

First, I place a document on display in its own terms, examining the text in particular and in its full particularity and immediacy. Here I want to describe the text from three perspectives: rhetoric, logic, and topic (the standard program of literary criticism in the age at hand). Reading documents one by one represents a new approach in the study of a Judaism. Ordinarily, people have composed studies by citing sayings attributed to diverse authorities without regard to the place in which these sayings occur. They have assumed that the sayings really were said by those to whom they are attributed, and, in consequence, the generative category is not the document but the named authority. But if we do not assume that the documentary lines are irrelevant and that the attributions are everywhere to be taken at face value, then the point of origin – the document – defines the categorical imperative, the starting point of all study.

Second, I seek to move from the text to that larger context suggested by the traits of rhetoric, logic, and topic. Here I want to compare one text to others of its class and ask how these recurrent points of emphasis, those critical issues and generative tensions, draw attention from the limits of the text to the social world that the text's authorship proposed to address. Here, too, the notion that a document exhibits traits particular to itself is new with my work, although, overall, some have episodically noted traits of rhetoric distinctive to a given document, and, on the surface, differences as to topic – observed but not explained – have been noted. Hence the movement from text to context and how it is effected represents a fresh initiative on my part.

Finally, so far as I can, I want to find my way outward toward the matrix in which a variety of texts find their place. In this third stage I want to move from the world of intellectuals to the world they proposed to shape and create. That inquiry defines as its generative question how the social world formed by the texts as a whole proposes to define and respond to a powerful and urgent question, that is, I want to read the canonical writings as response to critical and urgent questions. Relating documents to their larger political settings is not a commonplace, and, moreover, doing so in detail – with attention to the traits of logic, rhetoric, and topic – is still less familiar.

Writings such as those in the Judaic canon of the dual Torah have been selected by the framers of a religious system, and, read all together, those writings are deemed to make a cogent and important statement of that system, hence the category, "canonical writings." Now let us revert to my opening remarks of a more theoretical nature concerning the systemic study of a religion, in this example, a Judaism. I call that encompassing, canonical picture a "system," when it is composed of three necessary components: an account of a world view, a prescription of a corresponding way of life, and a definition of the social entity that finds definition in the one and description in the other. When those three fundamental components fit together, they sustain one another in explaining the whole of a social order, hence constituting the theoretical account of a system. Systems defined in this way work out a cogent picture, for those who make them up, of *how* things are correctly to be sorted out and fitted together, of *why* things are done in one way, rather than in some other, and of *who* they are that do and understand matters in this particular way. When, as is commonly the case, people invoke God as the foundation for their world view, maintaining that their way of life corresponds to what God wants of them, projecting their social entity in a particular relationship to God, then we have a religious system. When, finally, a religious system appeals as an important part of its authoritative literature or canon to the Hebrew Scriptures of ancient Israel or "Old Testament", we have a Judaism.

Now that we have focused upon the central role of specific documents, let me explain the movement from text to context and matrix that is signalled – once more – by use of the word "system." For reading a text in its context and as a statement of a larger matrix of meaning, I propose to ask larger questions of systemic description of a religious system represented by the particular text and its encompassing canon. Colleagues who work on issues of religion and society will find familiar the program I am trying to work out. But, I emphasize, the success of that program is measured by its power to make the texts into documents of general intelligibility for the humanities, to read the text at hand in such a way as to understand its statement within, and of, the human condition. That seems to me not only the opposite of reductionism but also a profoundly rationalist mode of inquiry.

Systems begin in the social entity, whether one or two persons or two hundred or ten thousand – there and not in their canonical writings, which come only afterward, or even in their politics. The social group, however formed, frames the system, the system then defines its canon within, and addresses the larger setting, the *polis* without. We describe systems from their end products, the writings. But we have then to work our way back from canon to system, not to imagine either that the canon is the system, or that the canon creates the system. The canonical writings speak, in particular, to those who can hear, that is, to the members of the community, who, on account of that perspicacity of hearing, constitute the social entity or systemic community. The community then comprises that social group the system of which is recapitulated by the selected canon. The group's exegesis of the canon in terms of the everyday imparts to the system the power to sustain the community in a reciprocal and self-nourishing process. The community through its exegesis then imposes continuity and unity on whatever is in its canon.

While, therefore, we cannot account for the origin of a successful system, we can explain its power to persist. It is a symbolic transaction, as I said just now, in which social change comes to expression in symbol change. That symbolic transaction, specifically, takes place in its exegesis of the systemic canon, which, in literary terms, constitutes the social entity's statement of itself So, once more, the texts recapitulate the system. The system does not recapitulate the texts. The system comes before the texts and defines the canon. The exegesis of the canon then forms that ongoing social action that sustains the whole. A system does not recapitulate its texts, it selects and orders them. A religious system imputes to them as a whole cogency, one to the next, that their original authorships have not expressed in and through the parts, and through them a religious system expresses its deepest logic, *and it also frames that just fit that joins system to circumstance.*

The issue of why a system originates and survives, if it does, or fails, if it does, by itself proves impertinent to the analysis of a system but of course necessary to our interpretation of it. A system on its own is like a language. A language forms an example of language if it produces communication through rules of syntax and verbal arrangement. That paradigm serves full well however many people speak the language, or however long the language serves. Two people who understand each other form a language community, even, or especially, if no one understands them. So too by definition religions address the living, constitute societies, frame and compose cultures. For however long, at whatever moment in historic time, a religious system always grows up in the perpetual present, an artifact of its day, whether today or a long-ago time. The only appropriate tense for a religious system is the present. A religious system always *is*, whatever it was, whatever it will be. Why so? Because its traits address a condition of humanity in society, a circumstance of an hour – however brief or protracted the hour and the circumstance.

When we ask that a religious composition speak to a society with a message of the *is* and the *ought* and with a meaning for the everyday, we focus on the power of that system to hold the whole together: the society the system addresses, the individuals who compose the society, the ordinary lives they lead, in ascending order of consequence. And that system then forms a whole and well-composed structure. Yes, the structure stands somewhere, and, indeed, the place where it stands will secure for the system either an extended or an ephemeral span of life. But the system, for however long it lasts, serves. And that focus on the eternal present justifies my interest in analyzing why a system works (the urgent agenda of issues it successfully solves for those for whom it solves those problems) when it does, and why it ceases to work (loses self-evidence, is bereft of its "Israel," for example) when it no longer works. The phrase, the *history* of a *system*, presents us with an oxymoron. Systems endure – and their classic texts with them – in that eternal present that they create. They evoke precedent, they do not have a history. A system relates to context, but, as I have stressed, exists in an enduring moment (which, to be sure, changes all the time). We capture the system in a moment, the worm consumes it an hour later. That is the way of mortality, whether for us one by one, in all mortality, or for the works of humanity in society. But systemic analysis and interpretation requires us to ask questions of history and comparison, not merely description of structure and cogency. So in this exercise we undertake first description, that is, the text, then analysis, that is, the context, and finally, interpretation, that is, the matrix, in which a system has its being.

This brings me to the critical issue of the role of the systemic analysis of religion within the life of intellect. To me, that life is lived in learning and in teaching. Let me define matters, therefore, in terms of the world I know, the university. I see two important results for the teaching of religion as an academic subject. First, I am trying to learn how to read a text in such a way as to highlight the human situation addressed by an authorship. If I can do so, I can show undergraduates of diverse origin what this text has to say to people in general, not only to Jews (of a quite specific order) in particular. In other words, my entire enterprise is aimed at a humanistic and academic reading of classics of Judaism, yet with full regard for their specific statements to their own world. People wrote these books as a way of asking and answering questions we can locate and understand – that is my premise – and when we can find those shared and human dimensions of documents, we can relate classic writings to a world we understand and share. That imputes a common rationality to diverse authorships and ages – theirs and ours – and, I believe, expresses the fundamental position of the academic humanities.

The second lesson draws us from text to context. Treating a religion in its social setting, as something a group of people do together, rather than as a set of beliefs and opinions, prepares colleagues to make sense of a real world of ethnicity and political beliefs formed on the foundation of religious origins. Indeed, if colleagues do not understand that religion constitutes one of the formative forces in the world today, they will not be able to cope with the future. But how to see precisely the ways in which religion forms social worlds? In the small case of Judaism, a set of interesting examples is set forth. Here they see that diverse Judaic systems responded to pressing social and political questions by setting forth cogent and (to the believers) self-evidently valid answers. That is one important aspect of the world-creating power of religion, and one nicely illuminated in the formation of Judaic systems.

The more critical academic issue should be specified. We are living in an age in which the old humanities are joined by new ones; women's studies (in their humanistic mode), black studies, Jewish studies, and a broad variety of other subjects enter the curriculum. The universities require them, because we now know that the humanities encompass a world beyond the European, religions in addition to the Christian, for instance. But how are we to make our own and academic what appears at first encounter to be alien and incomprehensible? One solution accepts as special and particular the new humanities, treating as general and normal the old ones. Hence – in the settlement accepted by some – Jews teach Jewish things to Jews, and form a segregated intellectual community within the larger academic world. But I think that the subject matter at hand is too urgent and important – and altogether too interesting – to be left to the proprietors or to be permitted to be segregated.

To deprive interested colleagues and students of access to the rich human experience and expression contained within the cultural artifacts of hitherto excluded parts of humanity diminishes the academic program and misrepresents the condition of humanity. But how to afford access to what is strange and perceived as abnormal is not readily explained. I have spent nearly thirty years trying to find appropriate access for colleagues and students alike to one of the new humanities. In the terms of Judaic studies I have insisted that the ghetto walls, once down, may not be reconstructed in the community of intellect. And, in that same framework, I have spent my life trying to explore the dimensions of a world without walls. That is the context in which the entire program now spelled out finds its shape and motivation.

Chapter Two

The Systemic Analysis of Religion
in Theory and in Practice

Religions form social worlds and do so through the power of their rational thought, that is, their capacity coherently to explain data in a (to an authorship) self-evidently valid way. The framers of religious documents answer urgent questions, framed in society and politics to be sure, in a manner deemed self-evidently valid by those addressed by the authorships at hand. For at stake in this *ouevre* is a striking example of how people explain to themselves who they are as a social entity. Religion as a powerful force in human society and culture is realized in society, not only or mainly in theology; religion works through the social entity that embodies that religion. Religions form social entities – "churches" or "peoples" or "holy nations" or monasteries or communities – that, in the concrete, constitute the "us," as against "the nations" or merely "them." And religions carefully explain, in deeds and in words, who that "us" is – and they do it every day. To see religion in this way is to take religion seriously as a way of realizing, in classic documents, a large conception of the world.

But how do we describe, analyze and interpret a religion, and how do we relate the contents of a religion to its context? These issues of method are worked out through the reading of texts, and, I underline, through taking seriously and in their own terms the particularity and specificity of texts. This I accomplish by special reference to problems in studying Judaism in particular. Here I offer an account of the theory and practice of the systemic analysis of religion, as I have worked out how to conduct such an analysis in the case of Judaism.

I. Issue of Theory: Religion as Tradition or as System

Religion may represent itself as a tradition, meaning, the increment of the ages. Or it may come forth as a cogent statement, a well-crafted set of compelling answers to urgent questions. A religious tradition covers whatever the received sedimentary process has handed on. A religious system addresses in an orderly way a world view, a way of life, and a defined social entity. And both processes of thought, the traditional or the systematic, obey, each its own rules. The life of intellect may commence morning by morning. Or it may flow from an ongoing process of thought, in which one day begins where yesterday left off, and one generation takes up the task left to it by its predecessors. A system of thought by definition starts fresh, defines first principles, augments and elaborates them in balance, proportion, above all, logical order. In a traditional process, by contrast, we never start fresh but only add, to an ongoing increment of knowledge, doctrine, and mode of making judgment, our own deposit as well. And, in the nature of such an ongoing process, we never start fresh, but always pick and choose, in a received program, the spot we choose to augment. The former process, the systematic one, begins from the beginning and works in an orderly, measured and proportioned way to produce a cogent, and neatly composed statement, a philosophy for instance. Tradition by its nature is supposed to describe not a system, whole and complete, but a process of elaboration of a given, received truth: exegesis, not fresh composition. And, in the nature of thought, what begins in the middle is unlikely to yield order and system and structure laid forth *ab initio*. In general terms, systematic thought is philosophical in its mode of analysis and explanation, and traditional thought is historical in its manner of drawing conclusions and providing explanations.

System and tradition as modalities of religious world-construction not only describe incompatible modes of thought but also generate results that cannot be made to cohere, in the aggregate, with one another. For the conflict between tradition and system requires us to choose one mode of thought about one set of issues and to reject the other mode of thought and also the things about which thought concerns itself. And that choice bears profound consequences for the shape of mind. So far as "tradition" refers to the matter of process, it invokes, specifically, an incremental and linear process that step by step transmits out of the past statements and wordings that bear authority and are subject to study, refinement, preservation, and transmission. In such a traditional process, by definition, no one starts afresh to think things through. Each participant in the social life of intellect makes an episodic and ad hoc contribution to an agglutinative process, yielding, over time, (to continue the geological metaphor) a sedimentary deposit. The opposite process we may call systematic, in that, starting as if from the very beginning and working out the fundamental principles of things, the intellect, unbound by received perspectives and propositions, constructs a free-standing and well-proportioned system. In terms of architect the difference is between a city that just grows and one that is planned; a scrapbook and a fresh composition; a composite commentary and a work of philosophical exposition.

The one thing a traditional thinker in religion, as against a system-builder in religion, knows is that he or she stands in a long process of thought, with the sole task of refining and defending received truth. And the systematic thinker affirms the task of starting fresh, seeing things all together, all at once, in the right order and proportion, a composition, not merely a composite, held together by an encompassing logic. A tradition requires exegesis, a system, exposition.

A tradition demands the labor of harmonization and elaboration of the given. A system begins with its harmonies in order and requires not elaboration but merely a repetition, in one detail after another, of its main systemic message. A tradition does not repeat but only renews received truth; a system always repeats because it is by definition encompassing, everywhere saying one thing, which, by definition, is always new. A system in its own terms has no history; a tradition defines itself through the authenticity of its history.

In the case of Judaism, it is universally acknowledged, we deal not with a system but with a tradition, and Judaism is invariably described as a traditional religion. And there can be no doubt that, from the Talmud of Babylonia, a.k.a. the Bavli, ca. A.D. 600, onward, the Jewish intellect flowed along traditional lines, making its contribution, from generation to generation, as commentary, not fresh composition. Every available history of Jewish thought, academic and vulgar alike, represents the principal modality of intellect as the refinement, adaptation, or adjustment of a received increment of truth. However new and lacking all precedent, Judaic systems find representation as elaborations of received Torah, imputed to verses of Scripture, and not as a sequence of fresh and original beginnings of systematic and orderly statements of well-composed and cogent principles. As between the fresh and perfect classicism of the well-proportioned Parthenon and the confused and disorderly alleyways of the streets below, the Jewish intellect made its residence in the side-alleys of the here and now, in an ongoing, therefore by definition never-neatly-constructed piazza.[1] The Jewish intellect carried on its work through receiving and handing on, not through thinking through in a fresh and fundamental way, the inheritance of the ages. It sought to preserve the sediment of truth and add its layer, not to dig down to foundations and build afresh, even bound to using the dirt removed in the digging. But is that how things were in the classical age, from the formation of the Pentateuch to the closure of the Bavli? That is to say, was the Jewish intellect in that formative age fundamentally traditional and historical, or essentially systematic and philosophical? At stake in the answer to that question is our fundamental characterization of the Jewish intellect, in its successive writings, in ancient times. From the viewpoint of offering a theoretical account of the description of systemic and against traditional thinking, the criteria for answering that question require specification.

---

[1]In so stating, of course, I bypass the philosophical movement that began with Saadya and ended four hundred years later. But the mainstream of Jewish intellectual life flowed not through speculative philosophy but through the parallel paths of study of the Bavli and its problems, on the one side, and speculation in the Qabbalah, on the other, and both of these were incremental and exegetical in structure and in form. They did not – by definition – begin afresh from generation to generation in the work of system-builders but persisted through the exercise of amplification, adapatation, renewal through reconsideration, and similar quintessentially traditional modes of thought.

We shall know the answer in two ways, the one formal, the other conceptual. The first, the merely formal, of course is the simpler. When an authorship extensively cites received documents and makes its statement through citing or clearly alluding to statements in those documents, then, on the face of it, that authorship wishes to present its ideas as traditional. It claims through its chosen form of expression (merely) to continue, (only) to amplify, extend, apply truth received, not to present truth discovered and demonstrated. That authorship then proposes to present its ideas as incremental, secondary, merely applications of available words. Not only so, but that authorship always situates itself in relationship to a received document, in the case of all Judaisms, of course, in relationship to the Pentateuch.[2] The second indicator, the conceptual, is the more subtle but also the more telling. When an authorship takes over from prior documents the problem and program worked out by those documents, contributing secondary improvements to an established structure of thought, then we may confidently identify that authorship as derivative and traditional. We realize that that is how matters were represented, in theory at least, by the framers of The Fathers, the opening statement of which is: "Moses received Torah at Sinai and handed it on to Joshua."[3] Then a piece of writing stands in a chain of handing on and receiving, handing on and receiving, in the context of a Judaism, of course, from Sinai.

But what sort of indicator tells us that we have a system, not a tradition? A systematic, and by nature, philosophical, statement or document, by contrast, presents its ideas as though they began with its author or authorship, rather than alluding to, let alone citing in a persistent way, a prior writing, e.g., Scripture. The form of a systematic statement ordinarily will be autonomous[4]. The order of discourse will begin from first principles and build upon them. The presentation of a system may, to be sure, absorb within itself a given document, citing its materials here and there. But – and this forms the indicator as to conception, not form alone – the authorship in such a case imposes its program and its problem upon received materials, without the pretense that the program

---

[2]Two authorships, those of the Pentateuch itself and of the Mishnah in no way pretended to relate to prior authorities but presented their own ideas in their own language and for their own purposes. The situation among the Essenes of Qumran is not so clear, because we do not have a systemic statement from their library. The Bavli's authorship took the route of imputing to origins in tradition what was, in fact, its own autonomous system, and the Bible's redactors, for their part, took received writings, hence traditions, and imputed to them the standing of a system.

[3]That theoretical statement of the traditional character of "Torah" of course contradicts the actualities of the document, the Mishnah, the origin and authority of which The Fathers is supposed to explain, but that fact does not concern us here.

[4]The exception is the Bavli, the authorship of which presents its system in the form of a commentary to the Mishnah and to Scripture.

and order of those inherited ("traditional" "authoritative" "scriptures") has made any impact whatsoever upon its presentation. An instance of a systematic statement's use of received materials is Matthew chapter two, which wishes to make the point that the events in the early years of Jesus's life fulfilled the promises of prophecy. That point requires the authorship to cite various verses; these are, of course, chosen for the occasion, and there is no pretense at a reading of whole passages in their "own" terms[5] and in accord with their "own" momentum of meaning. The Matthean authorship, rather, makes its point, which is part of its larger program and polemic, through an incidental, if important, allusion to prophecy.

The basic criterion of the systematic character of a document or statement, however, derives from a quite distinct trait. It is the authorship's purpose and whether, and how, a statement serves that purpose. How do we know that a statement, a sizable composition for instance, is meant to be systematic? In a well-composed system, every detail will bear the burden of the message of the system as a whole. Each component will make, in its terms, the statement that the system as a whole is intended to deliver. In order to understand that fact, we have to appreciate an important distinction in the analysis of systems. It is between a fact that is systemically vital, and one that is inert. For the study of economics, this point has been made by Joseph A. Schumpeter as follows: "In economics as elsewhere, most statements of fundamental facts acquire importance only by the superstructures they are made to bear and are commonplace in the absence of such superstructures."[6] That is to say, a system of religious thought, comprising a world view, a way of life, and a definition of the social entity meant to adopt the one and embody the other, makes ample use of available facts. In order to make their statement, the authors of the documents of such a system speak in a language common to their age. Some of these facts form part of the background of discourse, like the laws of gravity. They are, if important, inert, because they bear no portion of the burden of the systemic message. I call such facts inert. Other of these facts form centerpieces of the system; they may or may not derive from the common background. Their importance to the system forms part of the statement and testimony of that system.

Now in a well-composed system, every systemically generative fact will bear in its detail the message of the system as a whole, and, of course, inert facts will not. What I mean is simply illustrated. It is clear to any reader of Plato's *Republic,* Aristotle's *Politics* (and related corpus, to be sure), the Mishnah, or Matthew's *Gospel,* that these writers propose to set forth a complete account of the principle or basic truth concerning their subject, beginning, middle, and end. Accordingly, they so frame the details that the main point is repeated

---

[5]Whatever that can have meant in context!
[6]Joseph A. Schumpeter, *History of Economic Analysis,* p. 54.

throughout. At each point in the composition, the message as a whole, in general terms, will be framed in all due particularity. The choices of topics will be dictated by the requirements of that prevailing systemic attitude and statement. We can even account, ideally, for the topical components of the program, explaining (in theory at least) why one topic is included and another not. A topic will find its place in the system because only through what is said about that *particular* topic the system can make the statement it wishes to make.[7] Silence on a topic requires explanation, as much as we must supply a systemic motive or reason for the selection of, and substantial disquisition on, some other topic.

My criterion for whether a document is traditional or systematic, therefore systemic viewed as a construction, therefore allows us to test our judgment by appeal to facts of verification or falsification.[8] For the importance of recognizing the systemically generative facts is simple. When we can account for both inclusion and exclusion, we know not merely the topical program of the system but its fundamental intent and method, and we may assess the system-builders' success in realizing their program. A well-composed system will allow us to explain what is present and what is absent, as I said. Consequently, we may come to a reasonable estimation of the system's coverage, its realization of its program and full, exhaustive, presentation of its encompassing statement. Not only so, but a well-crafted systemic statement will by definition form a closed system, and the criterion of whether or not a statement stands on its own or depends upon other sources, e.g., information not contained within its encompassing statement but only alluded to by that statement, serves a a second major indicator for taxonomic purposes. Let me spell this out.

---

[7]That is the point of my *Economics of Judaism* (in press). Paul V. Flesher, *Oxen, Women, or Citizens? Slaves in the System of the Mishnah* (Atlanta: Scholars Press for Brown Judaic Studies, 1988) is able to demonstrate the same for the inclusion of slavery within the Mishnah's system. Flesher is able to point to a counterpart study by G. Vlastos, "Slavery in Plato's Republic," *Slavery in Classical Antiquity: Views and Controversies*, ed. M. I. Finley (Cambridge: Heffer, 1960), pp. 133-148, who shows how, in the system of Plato's *Republic*, slavery bears a systemic role and task. I should further point to Simon Schama's *Embarassment of Riches* (New York: Knopf, 1987) as an example of a systemic reading of detail. Schama's eye for the evocative visual symbol has given him the power to produce a masterpiece of cultural description, analysis, and interpretation.

[8]One example is the difficulty we face in classifying the writings of the Essene library of Qumran as a system at all. By contrast, we have no difficulty in representing the Mishnah as a systemic statement. I do not wish to enter into counterpart classification of Christian writings, e.g., Irenaeus, Origen, and Augustine, as to their traditional or systemic identification. I do maintain, that the Bible (Old and New Testaments together) forms a system and was meant to make a systemic statement, and that position rests on the function and purpose of the Bible as described in scholarship on the canon.

Some systems say precisely what they want on exactly those topics that make it possible to make its full statement. These are what we may call "closed systems,"[9] in that the authors tell us – by definition – everything that they want us to know, and – again, by definition – nothing that they do not think we need to know. They furthermore do not as a matter of systemic exposition have to refer us to any other writing for a further explication of their meaning (even though for reasons of argument or apologetic, they may do so). When an authorship sets forth a topic and completely and exhaustively expounds that topic, it has given us a systematic statement. The authorship has laid out its program, described the structure of its thought, given us what we need to know to grasp the composition and proportion of the whole, and, of course, supplied the information that, in detail, conveys to us the statement in complete and exhaustive form, thus, a closed system. It has done more than simply add a detail to available information. Quite to the contrary, the authorship of a statement of a closed system will frame its statement in the supposition that that authorship will tell us not only what we need to know, but everything we need to know, about a given topic. And that is a solid indicator of a systemic statement. An open system, by contrast, requires the recipient of a statement to refer not only to what an authorship tells us, but also to what an authorship invokes. The program is partial, the statement truncated, the system incomplete and not in correct composition and proportion, if, indeed, there is a system at all. That will then mark a traditional, not a systemic, statement. A piece of writing that depends upon other writings, and that is not occasioned by subjective judgment of the reader but by objective, if implicit, direction of the author, then forms part of an open system, or is not a systematic statement at all, but a fragment of thought.[10]

Now in all that I have said, I have treated as an axiom the formal and putative autonomy of systemic thought, which is so represented as if it begins *de novo* every morning, in the mind, imagination, and also conscience, of the system-builders. But what of what has gone before: other systems and their literary, as well as their social, detritus? Let us turn to the relationships to prior writings exhibited by systematic and traditional authorships, respectively. How do we know the difference between a system and a tradition in respect to the reception of received systems and their writings? The critera of difference are characterized very simply. A systematic authorship will establish connections to received writings, always preserving its own autonomy of perspective. A traditional authorship will stand in a relationship of continuity, commonly formal, but always substantive and subordinate, with prior writings. The

---

[9]On the Mishnah as a closed system, see my *Judaism: The Evidence of the Mishnah* (Second edition, augmented: Atlanta: Scholars Press for Brown Judaic Studies, 1988).

[10]True, such an open system may turn out to form part of a collage, but that is a different question.

authorship of a document that stands in a relationship of connection to prior writings will make use of their materials essentially in its own way. The authorship of a document that works in essential continuity with prior writings will cite and quote and refine those received writings but will ordinarily not undertake a fundamentally original statement of its own framed in terms of its own and on a set of issues defined separately from the received writings or formulations. The appeal of a systematic authorship is to the ineluctable verity of well-applied logic, practical reason tested and retested against the facts, whether deriving from prior authorities, or emerging from examples and decisions of leading contemporary authorities.

A traditional authorship accordingly will propose to obliterate lines between one document and another. A systematic authorship in the form of its writing ordinarily will not merge with prior documents. It *cites* the received writing as a distinct statement – a document "out there" – and does not merely allude to it as part of an internally cogent statement – a formulation of matters "in here." The systematic authorship begins by stating its interpretation of a received writing in words made up essentially independent of that writing, for example, different in language, formulation, syntax, and substance alike. The marks of independent, post facto, autonomous interpretation are always vividly imprinted upon the systematic authorship's encounter with an inherited document. Such a writing never appears to be represented by internal evidence as the extension of the text, in formal terms the uncovering of the connective network of relations, as literature a part of the continuous revelation of the text itself, in its material condition as we know it "at bottom, another aspect of the text." Not only so, but a systematic statement will not undertake the sustained imitation of prior texts by earlier ones. And even when, in our coming survey, we find evidence that, superficially, points toward a traditional relationship between and among certain texts that present us with closed systems and completed, systematic statements, we should, indeed, be struck by the independence of mind and the originality of authorships that pretend to receive and transmit, but in fact imagine and invent.

A traditional document (therefore the mind it represents) recapitulates the inherited texts; that defines the traditionality of such a writing. A systematic writing may allude to, or draw upon, received texts, but does not recapitulate them, except for its own purposes and within its idiom of thought. Traits of order, cogency, and unity derive from modes of thought and cannot be imposed upon an intellect that is, intrinsically, subordinated to received truth. A traditional writing refers back to, goes over the given. The system for its part not only does not recapitulate its texts, it selects and orders them, imputes to them as a whole cogency that their original authorships have not expressed in and through the parts, expresses through them its deepest logic. The system – the final and complete statement – does not recapitulate the extant texts. The antecedent texts – when used at all – are so read as to recapitulate the system.

The system comes before the texts and so in due course defines the canon. But in introducing the notion of canon, I have moved far beyond my story. At this point it suffices to claim that the thought processes of tradition and those of system building scarcely cohere. Where applied reason prevails, the one – tradition – feeds the other – the system – materials for sustained reconstruction.

The statement of a system is worked out according to the choices dictated by that authorship's sense of order and proportion, priority and importance, and it is generated by the problematic found by that authorship to be acute and urgent and compelling. When confronting the task of exegesis of a received writing, the authorship of a systematic statement does not continue and complete the work of antecedent writings within a single line of continuity ("tradition"). Quite to the contrary, that authorship makes its statement essentially independent of its counterpart and earlier document. In a systematic writing, therefore, the system comes first. The logic and principles of orderly inquiry take precedence over the preservation and repetition of received materials, however holy. The mode of thought defined, the work of applied reason and practical rationality may get underway.

First in place is the system that the authorship through its considered, proportioned statement as a whole expresses and serves in stupefying detail to define. Only then comes that selection, out of the received materials of the past, of topics and even concrete judgments, facts that serve the system's authorship in the articulation of its system. Nothing out of the past can be shown to have dictated the systematic program, which is essentially the work of its authorship. The tradition is ongoing, and that by definition. Then, also by definition, the system begins exactly where and when it ends. Where reason reigns, its inexorable logic and order, proportion, and syllogistic reasoning govern supreme and alone, revising the received materials and restating into a compelling statement, in reason's own encompassing, powerful, and rigorous logic, the entirety of the prior heritage of information and thought. From the Pentateuch to the Bavli, Judaic authorships presented not stages or chapters in an unfolding tradition but closed systems, each one of them constituting a statement at the end of a sustained process of rigorous thought and logical inquiry, applied logic and practical reason. The only way to read a reasoned and systematic statement of a system is defined by the rules of general intelligibility, the laws of reasoned and syllogistic discourse about rules and principles. And the correct logic for a systematic statement is philosophical and propositional, whether syllogistic or teleological. The way to read a traditional and sedimentary document by contrast lies through the *ad hoc* and episodic display of instances and examples, layers of meaning and eccentricities of confluence, intersection, and congruence. But I maintain that tradition and system cannot share a single throne, and a crown cannot set on two heads. Diverse statements of Judaisms upon examination will be seen to constitute not traditional but systemic religious documents, with a particular hermeneutics of order, proportion, above all, reasoned context, to tell us how to read each document. We cannot read these writings in accord with two incompatible hermeneutical programs, and, for reasons amply stated, I argue in favor of the philosophical and systemic, rather than the agglutinative and traditional, hermeneutics.

Whatever happens to thought, in the mind of the thinker ideas come to birth cogent, whole, complete – and on their own. Extrinsic considerations of context and circumstance play their role, but logic, cogent discourse, rhetoric – these enjoy an existence, an integrity too. If sentences bear meaning on their own, then to insist that sentences bear meaning only in line with their associates, their friends, companions, partners in meaning, contradicts the inner logic of syntax that, on its own, imparts sense to sentences. These are the choices: everything imputed, as against an inner integrity of logic and the syntax of syllogistic thought.[11]   But there is no compromise. As between the philosophical heritage of Athens and the hermeneutics of the Judaic tradition known from classical times forward, I maintain that one document of the Jewish intellect after another in classical times demonstrates the power of the philosophical reading of mind. In the end, the Jewish intellect in its classic age appealed to the self-evidence of truth compelled by of the well-framed argument, the well-crafted sentence of thought, the orderly cadence of correct, shared, and public logic – that and not the (mere) authority of tradition.

II. Viewing Religions as Systems

Before I focus upon the central role of specific documents, let me explain the movement I shall presently spell out, which is from text to context and matrix that is signalled by use of the word "system." For reading a text in its context and as a statement of a larger matrix of meaning, I propose to ask larger questions of systemic description of a religious system represented by the particular text and its encompassing canon. Colleagues who work on issues of religion and society will find familiar the program I am trying to work out. But the success of that program is measured by its power to make the texts into documents of general intelligibility for the humanities, to read the text at hand in such a way as to understand its statement within, and of, the human condition. That seems to me not only the opposite of reductionism but also a profoundly rationalist mode of inquiry.

Systems begin in the social entity, whether one or two persons or two hundred or ten thousand – there and not in their canonical writings, which come only afterward, or even in their politics. The social group, however formed,

---

[11]No one can maintain that the meanings of words and phrases, the uses of syntax, bear meanings wholly integral to discrete occasions. Syntax works because it joins mind to mind, and no one mind invents language, only gibberish. But that begs the question and may be dismissed as impertinent, since the contrary view claims far more than the social foundation of the language.

frames the system, the system then defines its canon within, and addresses the larger setting, the *polis* without. We describe systems from their end products, the writings. But we have then to work our way back from canon to system, not to imagine either that the canon is the system, or that the canon creates the system. The canonical writings speak, in particular, to those who can hear, that is, to the members of the community, who, on account of that perspicacity of hearing, constitute the social entity or systemic community. The community then comprises that social group the system of which is recapitulated by the selected canon. The group's exegesis of the canon in terms of the everyday imparts to the system the power to sustain the community in a reciprocal and self-nourishing process. The community through its exegesis then imposes continuity and unity on whatever is in its canon.

While, therefore, we cannot account for the origin of a successful religious-social system, we can explain its power to persist. It is a symbolic transaction, as I said just now, in which social change comes to expression in symbol-change. That symbolic transaction, specifically, takes place in its exegesis of the systemic canon, which, in literary terms, constitutes the social entity's statement of itself. So, once more, the texts recapitulate the system. The system does not recapitulate the texts. The system comes before the texts and defines the canon. The exegesis of the canon then forms that ongoing social action that sustains the whole. A system does not recapitulate its texts, it selects and orders them. A religious system imputes to them as a whole cogency, one to the next, that their original authorships have not expressed in and through the parts, and through them a religious system expresses its deepest logic, *and it also frames that just fit that joins system to circumstance.*

The whole works its way out through exegesis, and the history of any religious system – that is to say, the history of religion writ small – is the exegesis of its exegesis. And the first rule of the exegesis of systems is the simplest, and the one with which I conclude: *the system does not recapitulate the canon. The canon recapitulates the system.* The system forms a statement of a social entity, specifying its world view and way of life in such a way that, to the participants in the system, the whole makes sound sense, beyond argument. So in the beginning are not words of inner and intrinsic affinity, but (as Philo would want us to say) the Word: the transitive logic, the system, all together, all at once, complete, whole, finished – the word awaiting only that labor of exposition and articulation that the faithful, for centuries to come, will lavish at the altar of the faith. A religious system therefore presents a fact not of history but of immediacy, of the social present.

The issue of why a system originates and survives, if it does, or fails, if it does, by itself proves impertinent to the analysis of a system but of course necessary to our interpretation of it. A system on its own is like a language. A language forms an example of language if it produces communication through rules of syntax and verbal arrangement. That paradigm serves full well however many people speak the language, or however long the language serves. Two people who understand each other form a language community, even, or especially, if no one understands them. So too by definition religions address the living, constitute societies, frame and compose cultures. For however long, at whatever moment in historic time, a religious system always grows up in the perpetual present, an artifact of its day, whether today or a long-ago time. The only appropriate tense for a religious system is the present. A religious system always *is*, whatever it was, whatever it will be. Why so? Because its traits address a condition of humanity in society, a circumstance of an hour – however brief or protracted the hour and the circumstance.

When we ask that a religious composition speak to a society with a message of the *is* and the *ought* and with a meaning for the everyday, we focus on the power of that system to hold the whole together: the society the system addresses, the individuals who compose the society, the ordinary lives they lead, in ascending order of consequence. And that system then forms a whole and well composed structure. Yes, the structure stands somewhere, and, yes, the place where it stands will secure for the system either an extended or an ephemeral span of life. But the system, for however long it lasts, serves. And that focus on the eternal present justifies my interest in analyzing why a system works (the urgent agenda of issues it successfully solves for those for whom it solves those problems) when it does, and why it ceases to work (loses self-evidence, is bereft of its "Israel," for example) when it no longer works. The phrase, the *history* of a *system*, presents us with an oxymoron. Systems endure – and their classic texts with them – in that eternal present that they create. They evoke precedent, they do not have a history. A system relates to context, but, as I have stressed, exists in an enduring moment (which, to be sure, changes all the time). We capture the system in a moment, the worm consumes it an hour later. That is the way of mortality, whether for us one by one, in all mortality, or for the works of humanity in society. But systemic analysis and interpretation requires us to ask questions of history and comparison, not merely description of structure and cogency. So in this exercise we undertake first description, that is, the text, then analysis, that is, the context, and finally, interpretation, that is, the matrix, in which a system has its being.

III. Systemic Study of Religion in Practice: Studying Texts as Systemic Indicators

Let me now spell out in concrete terms how I have tried to read literary texts in the case of a Judaism as components of a system or as constituting on their own systemic statements. My work on the study of ancient Judaism has always proceeded in a systematic way, document by document. First, I place a document on display in its own terms, examining the text in particular and in its full particularity and immediacy. Here I describe the text from three perspectives: rhetoric, logic, and topic (the received program of literary criticism in the age at hand). Reading documents one by one represents a new approach in this field though it is commonplace in all other humanistic fields. Ordinarily, in studying ancient Judaism people have composed studies by citing sayings attributed to diverse authorities without regard to the place in which these sayings occur. They have assumed that the sayings really were said by those to whom they are attributed, and, in consequence, the generative category is not the document but the named authority. But if we do not assume that the documentary lines are irrelevant and that the attributions are everywhere to be taken at face value, then the point of origin – the document – defines the categorical imperative, the starting point of all study.

Second, I seek to move from the text to that larger context suggested by the traits of rhetoric, logic, and topic shared between one document and some other. Here I compare one text to others of its class and ask how these recurrent points of emphasis, those critical issues and generative tensions, draw attention from the limits of the text to the social world that the text's authorship proposed to address. Here too the notion that a document exhibits traits particular to itself is new with my work, although, overall, some have episodically noted traits of rhetoric distinctive to a given document, and, on the surface, differences as to topic – observed but not explained. Hence the movement from text to context and how it is effected represents a fresh initiative on my part.

Finally, so far as I can, I want to find my way outward toward the matrix in which a variety of texts find their place. In this third stage I want to move from the world of intellectuals to the world they proposed to shape and create. That inquiry defines as its generative question how the social world formed by the texts as a whole proposes to define and respond to a powerful and urgent question, that is, I read the canonical writings as response to critical and urgent questions. Relating documents to their larger political settings is not a commonplace, and, moreover, doing so in detail – with attention to the traits of logic, rhetoric, and topic – is still less familiar.

That brings us to the systemic approach, which, in this area, I have invented. Spelling it out is not difficult. Writings such as those of the Judaic canon have been selected by the framers of a religious system, and, read all together, those writings are deemed to make a cogent and important statement of that system, hence the category, "canonical writings." I call that encompassing, canonical picture a "system," *if and when* it is composed of three necessary components: an account of a world view, a prescription of a corresponding way of life, and a definition of the social entity that finds definition in the one and description in the other. When those three fundamental components fit together, they sustain one another in explaining the whole of a social order, hence constituting the theoretical account of a system. Systems defined in this way work out a cogent picture, for those who make them up, of *how* things are correctly to be sorted out and fitted together, of *why* things are done in one way, rather than in some other, and of *who* they are that do and understand matters in this particular way. When, as is commonly the case, people invoke God as the foundation for their world view, maintaining that their way of life corresponds to what God wants of them, projecting their social entity in a particular relationship to God, then we have a religious system. When, finally, a religious system appeals as an important part of its authoritative literature or canon to the Hebrew Scriptures of ancient Israel or "Old Testament," we have a Judaism.

I recognize that in moving beyond specific texts into the larger world view they join to present, I may be thought to cross the border from the humanistic study of classical texts to the anthropological reading of those same texts. I therefore emphasize that I take most seriously the particularity and specificity of each document, its program, its aesthetics, its logic. I do not propose to commit upon a classic writing an act of reductionism, reading a work of humanistic meaning merely as a sociological artifact. And, further, as between Weber and his critics, I take my place with Weber in maintaining that ideas constitute, in their context and circumstance, what sociologists call independent variables, not only responding to issues of society, but framing and giving definition to those larger issues. In this way I make a stand, in the systemic reading of the classic writings of Judaism in its formative age, with those who insist upon the ultimate rationality of discourse.

IV. Systemic Analysis in Concrete Context:
Explaining an *Ouevre*

The methodological problem that has occupied my mind since I completed my Ph.D. in 1960 therefore derives from my chosen discipline. It is history of religion, and my special area, history of Judaism in its formative period, the first six centuries A.D. I am trying to find out how to describe a Judaism in a manner consonant with the historical character of the evidence, therefore in the synchronic context of society and politics, and not solely or mainly in the diachronic context of theology which, until now, has defined matters. The inherited descriptions of the Judaism of the dual Torah (or merely "Judaism") have treated as uniform the whole corpus of writing called "the Oral Torah". The time and place of the authorship of a document played no role in our use of the allegations, as to fact, of the writers of that document. All documents have ordinarily been treated as part of a single coherent whole, so that anything we find in any writing held to be canonical might be cited as evidence of views on a given doctrinal or legal, or ethical topic. "Judaism" then was described by applying to all of the canonical writings the categories found imperative, e.g., beliefs about God, life after death, revelation, and the like. So far as historical circumstance played a role in that description, it was assumed that everything in any document applied pretty much to all cases, and historical facts derived from sayings and stories pretty much as the former were cited and the latter told.

Prior to the present time, ignoring the limits of documents, therefore the definitive power of historical context and social circumstance, all books on

"Judaism" or "classical," "Rabbinic," "Talmudic" Judaism, have promiscuously cited all writings deemed canonical in constructing pictures of the theology or law of that Judaism, severally and jointly, so telling us about Judaism, all at once and in the aggregate. That approach has lost all standing in the study of Christianity of the same time and place, for all scholars of the history of Christianity understand the diversity and contextual differentiation exhibited by the classical Christian writers. But, by contrast, ignoring the documentary origin of statements, the received pictures of Judaism have presented as uniform and unitary theological and legal facts that originated each in its own document, that is to say, in its distinctive time and place, and each as part of a documentary context, possibly also of a distinct system of its own. I had of course corrected that error by insisting that each of those documents be read in its own terms, as a statement – if it constituted such a statement – of a Judaism, or, at least, to and so in behalf of, a Judaism. I maintained that each theological and legal fact was to be interpreted, to begin with, in relationship to the other theological and legal facts among which it found its original location.

The result of that reading of documents as whole but discrete statements, as I believe we can readily demonstrate defined their original character, is five systemic studies of documents: *Judaism: The Evidence of the Mishnah, Judaism and Society: The Evidence of the Yerushalmi, Judaism and Scripture: The Evidence of Leviticus Rabbah,* as well as *Judaism and Story: The Evidence of The Fathers According to Rabbi Nathan.* At the conclusion of that work, for reasons spelled out in its own logic, I stated that the documentary approach had carried me as far as it could. I reached an impasse for a simple reason. Through the documentary approach I did not have the means of reading the whole all together and all at once. The description, analysis, and interpretation of a religious system, however, require us to see the whole in its entirety, and I had not gained such an encompassing perception. That is why I recognized that I had come to the end of the line, although further exercises in documentary description, analysis, and interpretation and systemic reading of documents assuredly will enrich and expand, as well as correct, the picture I have achieved in the incipient phase of the work.

I have worked on describing each in its own terms and context the principal documents of the Judaism of the dual Torah. I have further undertaken a set of comparative studies of two or more documents, showing the points in common as well as the contrasts between and among them. This protracted work is represented by systematic accounts of the Mishnah, tractate Avot, the Tosefta, Sifra, Sifré to Numbers, the Yerushalmi, Genesis Rabbah, Leviticus Rabbah, Pesiqta deRab Kahana, The Fathers According to Rabbi Nathan, the Bavli, Pesiqta Rabbati, and various other writings. In all of this work I have proposed to examine one by one and then in groups of afines the main components of the dual Torah. I wished to place each into its own setting and so attempt to trace the unfolding of the dual Torah in its historical manifestation. In the later stages of the work, I attempted to address the question of how some, or even all, of the particular documents formed a general statement. I wanted to know where and how documents combined to constitute one Torah of the dual Torah of Sinai.

Time and again I concluded that while two or more documents did intersect, the literature as a whole is made up of distinct sets of documents, and these sets over the bulk of their surfaces do not as a matter of fact intersect at all. The upshot was that while I could show interrelationships among, for example, Genesis Rabbah, Leviticus Rabbah, Pesiqta deRab Kahana, and Pesiqta Rabbati, or among Sifra and the two Sifrés, I could not demonstrate that all of these writings pursued in common one plan, defining literary, redactional, and logical traits of cogent discourse, or even one program, comprising a single theological or legal inquiry. Quite to the contrary, each set of writings demonstrably limits itself to its distinctive plan and program and not to cohere with any other set. And the entirety of the literature most certainly cannot be demonstrated to form that one whole Torah, part of the still larger Torah of Sinai, that constitutes the Judaism of the dual Torah.

Having begun with the smallest whole units of the Oral Torah, the received documents, and moved onward to the recognition of the somewhat larger groups comprised by those documents, I reached an impasse. On the basis of literary evidence – shared units of discourse, shared rhetorical and logical modes of cogent statement, for example – I came to the conclusion that a different approach to the definition of the whole, viewed all together and all at once, was now required. Seeing the whole all together and all at once demanded a different approach. But – and I state with heavy emphasis: *it has to be one that takes full account of the processes of formation and grants full recognition to issues of circumstance and context, the layers and levels of completed statements.* That is what I propose to accomplish in the exercise of systemic analysis. My explanation of the movement from text, to context, to matrix, now takes on, I believe, more concrete meaning. This comes to expression in two types of studies, one on the encompassing system yielded by a number of documents, in such works as *"Israel:" Judaism and its Social Metaphors,* (Philadelphia, 1988: Fortress Press) *The Incarnation of God: The Character of Divinity in Formative Judaism.* (Philadelphia, 1988: Fortress Press), and *Writing with Scripture: The Authority and Uses of the Hebrew Bible in the Torah of Formative Judaism.* (Philadelphia, 1989: Fortress Press [With William Scott Green]). The other sort of study leads me into the inquiry into those traits of mind in the system at hand that bear comparison to counterpart traits in other systems altogether. One aspect concerns logic, in my *The Making of the Mind of Judaism.* (Atlanta, 1987: Scholars Press for Brown Judaic Studies) and *The Formation of the Jewish Intellect. Making Connections and Drawing Conclusions in the Traditional System of Judaism* (submitted to The University of Chicago Press). The other has to do with asking about how a given system sets forth its ideas through discourse on commonly discussed problems such as economics and politics. In that context I have completed *The Economics of Judaism. The Initial Statement* (submitted to The University of Chicago Press) and plan to work on *The Politics of Judaism. The Formative Age.*

My entire enterprise is aimed – for reasons given in the Preface – at a humanistic and academic reading of classics of Judaism, yet with full regard for their specific statements to their own world. People wrote these books as a way of asking and answering questions we can locate and understand – that is my premise – and when we can find those shared and human dimensions of documents, we can relate classic writings to a world we understand and share. That imputes a common rationality to diverse authorships and ages – theirs and ours – and, I believe, expresses the fundamental position of the academic humanities. I am therefore drawn from text to context. Treating a religion in its social setting, as something a group of people do together, rather than as a set of beliefs and opinions, prepares colleagues to make sense of a real world of ethnicity and political beliefs formed on the foundation of religious origins. Indeed, if colleagues do not understand that religion constitutes one of the formative forces in the world today, they will not be able to cope with the future. But how to see precisely the ways in which religion forms social worlds? In the small case of Judaism, a set of interesting examples is set forth. Here they see that diverse Judaic systems responded to pressing social and political questions by setting forth cogent and (to the believers) self-evidently valid answers. That is one important aspect of the world-creating power of religion, and one nicely illuminated in the formation of Judaic systems.

The critical, narrowly academic issue should now be specified, since it allows me to conclude where I began, with the particular but also exemplary problem of my own academic and scholarly career. We are living in an age in which the old humanities are joined by new ones; women's studies (in their humanistic mode), black studies, Jewish studies, and a broad variety of other subjects enter the curriculum. The universities require them, because we now know that the humanities encompass a world beyond the European, religions in addition to the Christian, for instance. But how are we to make our own and academic what appears at first encounter to be alien and incomprehensible? One solution accepts as special and particular the new humanities, treating as general and normal the old ones. Hence – in the settlement accepted by some – Jews teach Jewish things to Jews, and form a segregated intellectual community within the larger academic world. But I think that the subject matter, religion, is too urgent and important – and altogether too interesting – to be left to the proprietors or to be permitted to be segregated. To deprive interested colleagues and students of access to the rich human experience and expression contained within the cultural artifacts of hitherto excluded parts of humanity diminishes the academic program and misrepresents the condition of humanity.

But how to afford access to what is strange and perceived as abnormal is not readily explained. I have spent nearly thirty years trying to find appropriate access for colleagues and students alike to one of the new humanities. In the terms of Judaic studies – as others have addressed black and women's studies and other components of the new humanities – I have insisted that the ghetto walls, once down, may not be reconstructed in the community of intellect. And, in that same framework, I have spent my life trying to explore the dimensions of a world without walls. That is the context in which the entire program now spelled out, and the scholarly *ouevre* that has resulted, finds shape, draws motivation, make sense.

Chapter Three

Pentateuchal Judaism as a Religious System

The Pentateuch, that is, the Five Books of Moses, forms the first systemic statement in the history of Judaism.[1] For, as we review the canonical Scriptures of ancient Israel, known, for Christianity as the Old Testament, and for Judaism as the Written Torah or Tanakh (made up of T, N and K, standing for the first letters of these words: *Torah,* the Pentateuch, *Nebiim*, prophets, and *Ketubim*, writings) or the Written Torah, we find that only one systematic statement reaches full expression, the one presented in the Pentateuch. There alone, among all of the canonical writings of ancient Israel, do we find a full and exhaustive statement of the way of life and world view of an "Israel."[2] We shall presently review precisely what question finds its answer in the system of Pentateuchal Judaism. For any systemic analysis must locate the generative problematic that gives a system its movement, defines its priorities, holds the whole together. As is characteristic of any well-crafted system, the whole of the pentateuchal writings, as they were finally arranged and put together, is so aimed at making a single cogent statement. Only when we can identify that statement shall we find

---

[1]Strictly speaking: in the histories of Judaisms. I have spelled out these matters in my *First Principles of Systemic Analysis. Studies in the Case of Judaism* (Atlanta: Scholars Press for Brown Judaic Studies, 1987).

[2]Other biblical books refer to, or take for granted, systemic structures. But none of them presents a closed system, covering ethos, ethics, and social entity, seeing the whole all together and all at once, and, further, forming of the whole a self-evidently valid answer to a compelling question. By that criterion, only Ezekiel 40-48 comes close, but not by much. The other prophetic books and all of the writings make no pretense; they form a library, not a system, much in the model of the Essene library of Qumran. And forming them all into a single "book," called "the Bible," never took place. For when Christianity created "the Bible," it took up both "the Old Testament" and "the New Testament," and, like Christianity, Judaism, for its part, in the Judaism of the dual Torah, never recognized the ancient Israelite Scriptures as an autonomous statement on its own, but only as a component of the Torah, that is, the written component of the dual Torah of Sinai. The conception of "the Hebrew Scriptures" as a free-standing Scripture sacred to "Judaism" had to wait for a hearing in the nineteenth century, and the use of the word "the Bible" to refer only to what Christians call "the Old Testament" is simply an error both in theology and in correct literary nomenclature. No Judaism has a "Bible," and no Christianity has a "Torah."

our way toward the inner structures that impart to that statement proportion, composition, logical relationship and – it follows – cogency. For the order of the formation of the intellect is from the whole to the parts. That is to say, the systemic statement defines the logic needed to make that statement. The manner of making connections and drawing conclusions does not percolate upward into the framing of the systemic statement.

Let us first consider my claim that, among all of the canonical writings of ancient Israel now before us, only the Pentateuch constitutes, and presents, a religious system, comprising a world view, a way of life, and a defined social entity meant to realize the ethos and ethics in concrete form. It is the simple fact that all other scriptural writings stand in relationship to that system *au fond*. They either are arranged in succession to, therefore in relationship with, that system, for example, the historical books, Joshua, Judges, Samuel, and Kings. Or they make no pretense at exhibiting a systemic character at all. In all other scriptural books we look in vain, for example, for a picture of how people are to live, of who they are as a social entity, of the way the world is composed and to be explained. The compilers of Jeremiah, the authors of Psalms, the collectors of Proverbs – these estimable circles in no way provide the prescription for an entire social world.

True, there is Ezekiel 40-48, the counterpart to the pentateuchal description in Leviticus of the cult. What we find, in a fragmentary way underlines the uniqueness as a systemic statement, within the Hebrew Scriptures, of the Pentateuch. While the Priestly Code and related writings go on to describe the world arrayed around the cult, Ezekiel 40-48 ignores by treating only by indirection and implicit judgment the enveloping web of social relationships defined in detail by the priestly authorship. Ezekiel attends by explicit statement only to the structure of society within, and in relationship to the cult itself; the detail is lacking. The statement of hierarchization expressed through the cult completed, everything else is left to inference. But a systemic statement invariably speaks blatantly, repetitiously, boringly, and explicitly, saying its message over and over again in innumerable ways, but never by mere inference. What Ezekiel 40-48 omits but the Priestly Code encompasses marks the frontier between a truncated, and merely suggestive, outline of what someone might wish to conceive and set forth and a systemic statement. That contrast explains why the Pentateuch as now put together, in the "Five Books of Moses," in fact, the pentateuchal mosaic, forms the only candidate for classification as a system, so far as I can discern, in the entire corpus of canonical prophecy.

Not only so, but the prophetic compilations, for instance, Isaiah, Jeremiah, the Second Isaiah, and Ezekiel, take for granted not only a society but also a social system. They appeal to both ethos and ethics, shared values and a common way of life. But they make no systemic statement. We could not define the religious system, the Judaism, set forth by, e.g., Jeremiah. We can only adumbrate the system that is the premise of his critique, and that is quite a different thing. For a sustained critique of a system is not a systemic statement but, like a vine on a trellis, simply lies heavy upon a system. Such a critique hardly permits us to impute to prophecy a conception of a social order that accounts for how things are, addressing the relationships and institutions of society, the conceptions that account for the origins and authority of those institutions and givenness of those relationships. Either proposing to criticize in the name of those shared values an incongruent reality, or offering in judgment upon the existing society an explicitly fictive account of a better system that will some day be realized within Israel through God's intervention, prophets never undertake the work of system-builders. They presuppose, they allude to, they depend upon, but they never compose and set forth a well-proportioned and complete composition of their "Israel," its world view and way of life, in the way in which the Pentateuchal compilers did after 586 and before 450 B.C. As to the Writings, read as statements meant to realize, in a social system, a well-composed statement and intent, these prove at best episodic. The books of Psalms, Proverbs, Job, Song of Songs, Lamentations, and the like address diverse circumstances. Ad hoc and free-standing, none can be set forth as systemic in content or in character.

But, read in the context of the age in which they were put together as a whole, that is, in the sixth century B.C. the Five Books of Moses, Genesis, Exodus, Leviticus, Numbers, and Deuteronomy, can. The history of the Pentateuch *as a systematic statement* begins with the ultimate formation into a cogent composite of diverse writings. Where those materials came from, for whom they spoke to begin with, what they meant prior to their restatement in the context and system they now comprise, define questions the answers to which have no bearing whatsoever upon the systemic analysis of those same writings.[3] For the system begins whole, and what system-builders do with received materials is whatever they wish to do with them. They do not recognize themselves as bound by prior and original authors' intent, and neither are we so bound in interpreting the outcome of the work of composition and (re)statement.

---

[3]True, we know as fact that these diverse writings form a mosaic, each of the parts originating in its own time and addressing its distinctive circumstance. But a review of the components, one by one, an account of the bits and pieces formed into J, E, P, and D, a history of the agglutinative process that made of J and E JE, that then joined D to the lot and that set P and its perspective over the whole – the entire outcome of biblical sciences play no role in the analysis of the systemic character of the pentateuchal mosaic. For in the end, the pieces of the mosaic fit together, and that is because some one fit them together. They are to be described as received, and not as they originated, in sherds and remnants of God only knows what. For the origins of the materials now set forth in a systematic way play no role whatsoever in the description, analysis, and interpretation of what has been made of those materials.

Read, therefore, as a continuous and also complete[4] statement, the pentateuchal mosaic forms a system with an origin (Eden, Sinai) but without a secular history (this king, that king), addressed to a present that has only a future, but no pertinent past. But even when read in that way, does the pentateuchal mosaic conform to the definition of a system just now given? And how shall we know? In the two requisite dimensions of such a definition, world view and way of life, it does, and in the other indicative trait of a system, social focus and intent, it does as well.

For the pentateuchal mosaic, composite though it is, has been so formed as to frame a question and answer that question, forming remarkably disparate materials into a statement of coherence and order.[5] The question that is answered encompasses a variety of issues, but it always is one question: who is Israel in relationship to the land? In the aftermath of 586, the "exile," followed by ca. 530, the "return to Zion," that question certainly demanded attention among those few whose families had both gone into exile and returned to Zion, and the pentateuchal mosaic was compiled by the priests among them in particular as an account of the temple, cult, and priesthood in the center and heart of the way of life, world view, and social entity of the particular "Israel" the priests proposed to make up. That explains why the question from beginning in Genesis to conclusion at the eve of entry into the land in Deuteronomy is, what are the conditions for the formation of the union of Israel with the enchanted land it is to occupy? It also accounts for the ineluctable and persuasive character of the answer, once again encompassing a variety of details: the pentateuchal "Israel," defined by genealogy, like the priesthood, formed the family become holy people, and that genealogical "Israel" possesses the land by reason of the covenant of its fathers-founders, Abraham, Isaac, and Jacob. That covenant is given detail and substance with the forming of the people at Sinai. Israel the people possesses the land not as a given but as a gift, subject to stipulations.

---

[4]The pentateuchal mosaic read as a whole forms the prime model of a closed system, describing as it does the world view, way of life, social entity, past, present, and future, from beginning to end, all together and in what is transparently a complete way. Details of rules, of course, are tacitly taken for granted; the structure as a whole is encompassing. That is why I claim we detail with a complete and therefore closed system. I claim that the Mishnah forms another closed system. What marks it as odd is that its authorship rarely sets any of its judgments into relationship with the pentateuchal Judaism and never answers, for the document as a whole, the question of the relationship to the Torah revealed by God to Moses at Sinai. It is not only a closed system, it is also a nearly entirely autonomous and free-standing one.

[5]A mark of a closed system is that everything is in the right place, so that, were we to put something in a position other than where it now stands, it would be incomprehensible and the system would fall out of kilter. That is, what I said about propositional discourse as a matter of logic, as against fixed association which bears no intrinsic sense of order, this, then that, pertains also to the analysis of the closed as against the open system.

The fundamental systemic statement repetitiously and in one detail after another[6] answers the question of why Israel has lost the land of Israel and what it must do to hold on to it once again. Accordingly, in a single statement we may set forth the systemic message: God made the land and gave it to Israel on condition that Israel do what God demands. That is the answer. It also leads us to define the ineluctable question, that demands this answer, the question that presses and urgently insists upon an answer. In the circumstance, after the destruction of the temple of Jerusalem in 586 B.C., of the formation of the pentateuchal composition and system, the question is equally accessible. It is, why has Israel lost the land, and what does Israel have to do now to hold on to it again?

The pentateuchal system, taking shape in the aftermath of the exile to Babylonia in 586 and reaching closure with the return to Zion some decades later finds urgent the question framed by that rather small number of Israelite families who remembered the exile, survived in Babylonia, and then, toward the end of the sixth and fifth centuries B.C., returned to Zion, knew things that enlandised Israel before 586 could never have imagined The system of Judaism that would predominate therefore began by making a selection of facts to be deemed consequential, hence historical, and by ignoring, in the making of that selection, the experiences of others who had a quite different perception of what had happened.[7] And, as a matter of fact, that selection of systemically important facts dictated the making of connections, that is, the joining of this fact to that fact, rather than to some other. For once the system-builders know the facts they wish to address, they also will discern connections between those facts and no others. The logic of connection depends upon the logic of drawing conclusions from connection. And conclusions derive from a prior recognition of questions we wish to answer. For one example, I may posit, by way of a mental experiment, a simple case: the connection between the destruction of the temple, the exile to Babylonia, and the return to Zion, will not have struck a family that remained in Babylonia as self-evident; for that family did not return to Zion. To the thought devoted to social circumstances, the return to Zion will have proved not an inevitable and ineluctable event, this, then that, this, joined to that. In such a system as it formed, that fact will have proved inert, hence not part of the joints of the construction as a whole.

That is why I claim that the connections deemed ineluctable began with the system, not with the details. The facts found noteworthy to begin with found consequence in the system that identified *those* facts and not other facts. And the

---

[6]I should like to say, "in *every* detail," but it is hardly essential for the point I wish to make. Not only so, but since the priestly redactors worked with received materials that they did not rewrite beginning to end, I suspect that such a claim of perfect consistency in all details to the main message would not stand. It suffices to assert, as I do, the thrust and direction of the whole and a large component of the parts.

[7]Here again we discern the footsteps of the system-builders.

one fact that the ones who came back, and, by definition, many of those who were taken away, were *priests* made all the difference, as the books of Ezra and Nehemiah indicate. For to the priests the fate of the temple defined what mattered in 586. The destruction of the Temple defined that web of social relationships and connections that joined one thing to something else and set the whole into hierarchical order. It had to follow, then, that what made the difference, what was at stake, "three generations later" was not alone the restoration of Israel to the land, but the rebuilding of the Temple. The former not connected to the latter made no sense. And that connection, people to land through temple, formed the generative problematic of the system as a whole, accounting, as a matter of fact, for the bulk of the materials included in the Pentateuch and for the way in which those materials are laid out. To the pentateuchal system the cult was the key, the temple (in mythic language then) the nexus between heaven and earth. The Five Books of Moses composed as its systemic statement an account of the unsettling encounter with annihilation avoided, extinction postponed, life renewed – temple restored as portrayed in P's Leviticus and Numbers. To Israel the Torah imparted the picture of society subject to judgment. And it was the priests' judgment in particular that prevailed.

What conclusion was to be drawn from that generative problem and definitive pattern of connection that the system put forth? It was that the system's "Israel's" life was, as I said, itself not a given but a gift. The system's "Israel" stood for a group that at any time might lose its land, so that the relation to the land,[8] the foundation of social existence was turned into the basis for and indicator of the group's moral existence as well. The principal givens of the pentateuchal Torah's systemic paradigm, namely, its "Israel's" heightened sense of its own social reality, its status as an elected people standing in a contractual or covenantal relationship with God, propositions of both the Torah and the historical and prophetic writings of the century beyond 586, in fact speak out of inner structure of the system. True, after millenia of repetition, we take for granted the givenness of the systemic propositions. But once they were fresh assertions, contradicting other views (which we can scarcely reconstruct) and answering burning questions. Accordingly, these systemic givens as a matter of fact express the system's logic, not a logic intrinsic in events, even in events selected and reworked. The givens frame the system's premises, not the data of Israel's common life in either Babylonia, to which they were simply irrelevant, or the Land of Israel, among those who never went into "exile," and who found themselves subject to the judgment of those who had gone and come back. For the system not only selected the events it would deem consequential. It also selected those events that would not form connections to one another and so

---

[8]Not merely what happened *in* the land, as with Amos, for example.

would not yield conclusions, and that would, therefore, prove, in an exact sense of the word, *inconsequential:* not connected and therefore not significant.

Let us dwell on this matter of a systemic judgment upon the given society, for it shows with great clarity the standing and viewpoint of the system-builders. Specifically, what we now understand is that the system-builders did not describe the given social world but proposed to create afresh, out of their own minds first of all, a society that should come to realization. From the perspective of a vast Israelite population, namely, Jews who had remained in the land, Jews who had never left Babylonia, Jews living in other parts of the world, such as Egypt, the system spoke of events that simply had never happened or had not happened in the way that the pentateuchal mosaic claims. For the systemic conclusions invoked no self-evidently valid connections, when people had no data out of their own, or their family's, experience, on the basis of which to make such connections. Consider the Jews who remained in the land after 586, or those who remained in Babylonia after Cyrus's decree permitting the return to Zion. For both groups, for different reasons, there was no alienation, also, consequently, no reconciliation, and the normative corresponded to the merely normal: life like any other nation, wherever it happened to locate itself. And that ignores Jews in Egypt, Mesopotamia, and other parts of the world of the time, who were not in the Land when it was captured and who also were not taken captive to Babylonia.

True enough, treating exile and return as the generative problematic and therefore as normative imparted to the exile the critical and definitive position. It marked Israel as special, elect, subject to the rules of the covenant and its stipulations. But, as we now realize, for much of Israel, some system other than the system of the normative alienation constructed by the Judaism of the Torah will have to have enjoyed that self-evidence that, for the (priestly) exiles returned, the system of the Torah possessed. For to them who stayed put, the urgent question of exile and return, the self-evidently valid response of election and covenant, bore slight relevance, asked no questions worth asking, provided no answers worth believing. When we want an example of a religious system creating a society, we can find few better instances than the power of the conception of Israel expressed by the Pentateuch and associated writings, of the period after 586 B.C., to tell people not only the meaning of what had happened but what had happened: to create for Israelite society a picture of what it must be and therefore had been.

That sense of heightened reality, that intense focus on the identification of the nation as extraordinary, represented only one possible picture of the meaning of events from 586 B.C. onward. But we do not have access to any other but the system of the Torah. And the system of the Torah after 586 did not merely describe things that had actually happened, systemically inert facts, so to speak, but made a choice among such inert or "normal" events, rendering some of them normative and mythic, turning an experience into a paradigm of experience. The system defined the events that mattered and, we now see clearly, therefore dictated the kinds of connections it would discern, and, it goes without saying, also, therefore, the conclusions it would draw. The systemic paradigm began as a paradigm, not as a set of actual events that people saw as connected and that they then transformed into a normative pattern. And the conclusions generated by the paradigm, it must follow, derived not from reflection on things that happened but from the logic of the paradigm. Accordingly, the system comes prior to the logic that forms its interior structure and defines its inner proportions and composition.[9]

What follows is simple. First came the system, its world view and way of life formed whole we know not where or by whom. Then came the selection, by the system, of consequential events and their patterning into systemic propositions. That is the point at which systemic logic enters. And finally, at a third stage (of indeterminate length of time) came the formation and composition of the canon that would express the logic of the system and state those "events" that the system would select or invent for its own expression. And that is the stage at which a self-conscious positioning of a system vis-à-vis inherited systems takes place. We have now dealt with the first two matters – the system and its consequent logic of making connections and drawing conclusions. Let us now turn to the issue of how the framers presented their work, specifically, whether or not the system-builders who made the pentateuchal Judaism presented their system as (merely) traditional or as a free-standing system. The answer to the question is not that they inherited and made use of available materials, "traditions." That is beside the point. What we want to know concerns the system, and not the raw materials of which it was composed, and that is a quite different matter. Specifically, does the pentateuchal authorship represent its work as a statement of a tradition, out of the long-ago past, or does it present its statement as an essentially autonomous statement, whole and complete on its own? That is the question at hand.

Like all religious systems, the fulcrum on which the pentateuchal Judaism rests is its social entity, the system's "Israel," and that "Israel" in the pentatuechal system refers not to a natural past, generations of descent family by family,[10] but an act of selection of one family and *its* descendants, a very different thing. Since, chief among the propositions of the system as the Torah

---

[9]Not only so, but that same paradigm would create expectations that could not be met, so would renew the resentment captured by the myth of exile, while at the same time setting the conditions for remission of resentment, so resolving the crisis of exile with the promise of return. This self-generating, self-renewing paradigm formed that self-fulfilling prophecy that all Judaisms have offered as the generative tension and critical symbolic structure of their systems. That is my argument in *Self-Fulfilling Prophecy. Exile and Return in the History of Judaism* (Boston: Beacon Press, 1987).

[10]And that is despite the polemic of Chronicles, for example.

of Moses defined it is the notion of the election of Israel effected in the covenant, we may say that, systemically speaking, Israel – the Israel of the Torah and historical-prophetic books of the sixth and fifth centuries – selected itself. The system created the paradigm of the society that had gone into exile and come back home, and, by the way, the system also cut its own orders, that contract or covenant that certified not election but self-selection. A particular experience, transformed by a religious system into a paradigm of the life of the social group, has become normative and therefore generative. But – to repeat the central point – that particular experience *itself* happened, to begin with, in the minds and imaginations of the authorship of the Pentateuch as we have it, not in the concrete life or in the politics and society of Israel in its land and in exile. The same is so for a long list of systemic givens, none of them, as a matter of fact, matters of self-evidence except to those to whom they were self-evident.

That is why a large portion of the Pentateuch devotes time and attention to the matter of the cult, that is to say, the centrality of sacrifice, the founding of the priesthood and its rules, and the importance of the Temple in Jerusalem. That is why many of the stories of Genesis are aimed at explaining the origin, in the lives and deeds of the patriarchs, of the locations of various cultic centers prior to the centralization of the cult in Jerusalem, the beginnings of the priesthood, the care and feeding of priests, the beginnings and rules of the sacrificial system, the contention between priestly castes, e.g., Levites and priests, and diverse other matters. Much of Exodus is devoted to the description of the tabernacle in the wilderness as prototype of the temple. Leviticus and much of Numbers are devoted to the same topic. Deuteronomy, the most compendious and encompassing of the composites, pays ample attention to the matter. But what is important is not the centrality of the cult to the systemic statement as a whole. Rather the system links the whole of the social order to the cult, and that is what imparts to the system its distinctive structure and conveys its urgent messages. The picture of the system's Israel, its "kingdom of priests" ruled by priests, its "holy people" living out the holiness imparted by obedience to the covenant, as a matter of fact laid claim to the authority of God's revelation to Moses at Sinai. But, of course, "Sinai" stood for Babylonia. There the priests drew together the elements of the received picture and reshaped them into the fairly coherent set of rules and narratives for the social order, the account of the social entity, "Israel," its way of life, its world view, that we now know as the Pentateuch. All of this is represented as given, revealed by God to Moses at Sinai. And nothing is presented as tradition formed out of a long chain of incremental and sedimentary formation. It was all together, all at once, one time, with no past other than the past made up for the system, not process, not justified by ancient custom. The ideology of the statement appeals to the opposite of tradition: revelation, of which pentateuchal Scripture is the exhaustive record, and that alone. I point, therefore, to the system's explanation of its own origins in a single act of revelation as the stunningly final judgment of its own character: not a (mere) tradition, preserved by mortals, but a system, a revelation, set forth by God to Moses once for all time. True, systems can and have set forth other indicators of their judgment of themselves, and they need not appeal to a one-time revelation to impute to themselves systemic and not traditional standing. But for the pentateuchal Judaism, the appeal to Sinai suffices to state the Judaism's definitive character as a system, not as a tradition in any sense the authorship at hand can have understood.[11]

This brings us to the center of matters, the system itself. If I am correct that the pentateuchal Judaism makes a statement, I should be able to repeat it in a simple and cogent way. We have in hand a most convenient statement of the systemic message as a whole. The priests' vision, attaching to the Pentateuchal system as a whole, is characterized as follows:

> In the priests' narrative the chosen people are last seen as pilgrims moving through alien land toward a goal to be fulfilled in another time and place, and this is the vision, drawn from the ancient story of their past, that the priests now hold out to the scattered sons and daughters of old Israel. They too are exiles encamped for a time in an alien land, and they too must focus their hopes on the promise ahead. Like the Israelites in the Sinai wilderness, they must avoid setting roots in the land through which they pass, for diaspora is not to become their permanent condition, and regulations must be adopted to facilitate this. They must resist assimilation into the world into which they are now dispersed, because hope and heart and fundamental identity lay in the future. Thus, the priestly document not only affirms Yahweh's continuing authority and action in the lives of his people but offers them a pattern for life that will ensure them a distinct identity.[12]

---

[11]The reader will rightly wonder why I insist that a systemic authorship take up a position on this question, which, after all, I have invented for my own analytical purposes. The answer becomes clear in the data to come, for two further groups of system-builders, those of the Mishnah and the Bavli, are very careful to identify themselves in relationship to other, prior systems, and to claim, or to avoid claiming, that they stand in a chain of tradition. If there is a single sentence in the pentateuchal mosaic that imputes to the system at hand the standing of a tradition handed on of old, rather than a revelation whole and complete, I cannot point to it. The paramount standing of Sinai as the explanation of the law, of God's instruction to Moses, who was to write everything down and hand it on with great precision, – that is what tells us how the authorship that invented the system wished the system to be understood. In secular language it is free-standing and autonomous, fresh this morning, so to speak. I pursue this issue in detail in my *Formation of the Jewish Intellect* (in press).

[12] W. Lee Humphreys, *Crisis and Story. Introduction to the Old Testament* (Palo Alto: Mayfield Publishing Co. , 1979), p. 217. I choose Humphreys's statement not only because of its authority, but also because it speaks for a considerable scholarly consensus, serving, after all, as a textbook account of what, in general, people now think.

The net effect of the pentateuchal vision of Israel, that is, its world view seen in the aggregate, lays stress on the separateness and the holiness of Israel, all the while pointing to dangers of pollution by the other, the outsider.

The way of life, with its stress on distinguishing traits of an Israel distinct from, and threatened by, the outsider corresponds. The fate of the nation, moreover, depends upon the loyalty of the people, in their everyday life, to the requirements of the covenant with God, so history forms the barometer of the health of the nation. In these ways the several segments of the earlier traditions of Israel were so drawn together as to make the point peculiarly pertinent to Israel in exile. It follows that the original Judaic system, the one set forth by the Pentateuch, answered the urgent issue of exile with the self-evident response of return. The question was not to be avoided, the answer not to be doubted. The center of the system, then, lay in the covenant, the contract that told Israel the rules that would govern: keep these rules and you will not again suffer as you have suffered. Violate them and you will. At the heart of the covenant was the call for Israel to form a kingdom of priests and a holy people.

That brings us back, via a circuitous route, to the matter of the logic of cogent discourse, that matter of principles of making connections and drawing conclusions that I have stressed as the inner building blocks of the Jewish intellect. The pentateuchal system clearly rejects the philosophical, and chooses the teleological approach to finding out how one thing links up with some other and to drawing conclusions from that connection. We know that the choice of types of facts for connection time and again falls upon what are deemed to be events, and, in consequence, the principal mode of sustained discourse is the telling of stories. The world view of the system emerges in particular through these stories. When the system-builders wish to account for the identification of the social entity, "Israel," they tell the story of the founders, the patriarchs and matriarchs, and what happened to them. "Israel" then comes into being through the story of how the family became the people. The laws of the system, its way of life, are set forth within a narrative setting, e.g., revelation at Sinai, in Exodus, the circumstance and the speaker and the authority, in Leviticus and Numbers. Not only so, but even where the laws are laid out essentially independent of narrative, as in Deuteronomy, the laws as a whole are laid out in a tight relationship to a story, so that the fictive setting provides what the system deems absolutely essential. In these and other instances we discern the system's general conception, that connection derives from sequence, first this, then that, hence that is because of this. Then the drawing of conclusions derives from connections discerned between this and that: one event, then another event, and the cause that links the latter to the former and explains the order of things.[13]

_____

[13]The observations here will take on considerable weight when we confront a different logic altogether, one in which connection rests not on teleology but on

From generalization we move to an instance of concrete speech. There we shall see that telological logic, dictating the connections we make and the conclusions we draw, appeals not only to history, though we entered that logic through the door of history. Teleology appeals to goal or purpose, of which history forms a mere example. What links together the sentences that follow is the goal stated at the outset. In achieving this goal, these are the things that one must do. Then a set of discrete sentences, not topically or logically related to one another at all, follows. And each sentence finds its place in context for the same reason. It is another way to achieve that purpose set forth at the head. Lev. 19:1-18 (given in the Revised Standard Version) provides our instance of teleological connection among otherwise unrelated facts/sentences:

And the Lord said to Moses, "Say to all the congregation of the people of Israel, You shall be holy, for I the Lord your God am holy.

"Every one of you shall revere his mother and his father and you shall keep my sabbaths, I am the Lord your God.

"Do not turn to idols or make for yourselves molten gods; I am the Lord your God.

"When you offer a sacrifice of peace offerings to the Lord, you shall offer it so that you may be accepted. It shall be eaten the same day you offer it or on the morrow, and anything left over until the third day shall be burned with fire. If it is eaten at all on the third day, it is an abomination, it will not be accepted, and every one who eats it shall bear his iniquity, because he has profaned a holy thing of the Lord; and that person shall be cut off from his people.

"When you reap the harvest of your land, you shall not reap your field to its very border, neither shall you gather the gleanings after your harvest. And you shall not strip your vineyared bare, neither shall you gather the fallen grapes of your vineyard; you shall leave them for the poor and for the sojourner. I am the Lord your God.

"You shall not steal, nor deal falsely, nor lie to one another. And you shall not swear by my name falsely and so profane the name of your God; I am the Lord. You shall not oppress your neighbor or rob him. The wages of a hired servant shall not remain with you all night until the morning. You shall not curse the deaf or put a stumbling block before the blind, but you shall fear your God; I am the Lord.

"You shall do no injustice in judgment; you shall not be partial to the poor or defer to the great, but in righteousness shall you judge your neighbor. You shall not go up and down as a slanderer among your people, and you shall not stand forth against the life of your neighbor; I am the Lord.

---

the inner logic of a topic and yields a conclusion not explaining history but setting forth a generalization concerning the world of society and nature. That systemic logic characterizes the thought of the framers of the Mishnah. I spell it out in my *Formation of the Jewish Intellect* (in press).

"You shall not hate your brother in your heart, but you shall reason with your neighbor, lest you bear sin because of him. You shall not take vengeance or bear any grudge against the sons of your own people, but you shall love your neighbor as yourself; I am the Lord."

Except for the opening and closing lines of the pericope, the linkage of fact to fact, the connection of sentence to sentence (treating the paragraphs as sentences), is hardly self-evident. These are all things that, unrelated to one another, relate to the goal of sanctification. This mixture of rules we should regard as cultic, as to sacrifice, moral, as to support of the poor, ethical, as to right-dealing, and above all religious, as to being "holy for I the Lord your God am holy" – the rules all together portray a complete and whole society: its world view, holiness in the likeness of God, its way of life, an everyday life of sanctification through the making of distinctions, its Israel: Israel. The definition of who is Israel lay at the foundation of the system, which was shaped to answer that urgent question of social explanation. That is what holds the whole together, and, we see, the principle of cogent discourse appeals to teleology expressed as a kind of narrative.[14]

But making connection in the teleological manner is not only dictated by the goals of an abstract order we have just reviewed. Connections link one event to another, one act to another, and, most important, an act to an event. Accordingly, the teleological logic of connection, and, necessarily, of conclusion as well, will appeal to what the framers conceive to be the ineluctable union between the actions of persons and the events that affect the society they form. "If you do this, that will happen," forms a statement linking an action to a social and historical result, and that forms, in another dimension, a teleological connection as well. Thus: "If you walk in my statutes and observe my commandments and do them, then I will give you your rains in their season" (Lev. 26:3), "But if you will not hearken to me and will not do all these commandments ... I will do this to you: I will appoint over you sudden terror...and you shall sow your seed in vain for your enemies shall eat it .... Then the land shall enjoy its sabbaths as long as it lies desolate while you are in your enemies' land ...." (Lev. 26:34). That teleology of connection and conclusion tells us what facts join what other facts, and what conclusions we are to draw in consequence. It is a uniform logic, and the structure of the pentateuchal intellect seems to me remarkably cogent.

---

[14]That is not to allege that the rules are in any sense narrative, but all of them, as a matter of fact, are set into a narrative context, and that is not only in general, that is, viewed as part of the Pentateuch as a whole, but also in detail. The authorship of the Mishnah did not find it necessary to provide its vast document with a narrative of any kind, and any teleological theory behind the Mishnaic Judaism is imputed by successor-writings. These are questions that carry us beyond the limits of this chapter. I have expanded on these matters in *The Formation of the Jewish Intellect*.

The pentateuchal system made its statement not only through the conclusions it set forth, but also through the processes of thought that after the fact generated these conclusions. It defined as its generative question the loss of the land and its restoration to and retention by Israel. It answered the question of how to prevent the events of the recent past from happening ever again. It gave as its answer the formation of a separate and holy society, an Israel. Events, the connections between and among them, the conclusions to be drawn from those connections, defined the focus of interest, because the system treated as urgent a question defined by what had happened to the "Israel" that the system chose to address. The Judaic system of the Pentateuch confronted the overwhelming question of the meaning of what had happened and supplied the (to the priests') self-evidently valid answer: Israel must obey the rules of holiness, and, if it does, then by keeping its half of the agreement or covenant, it could make certain God would find valid the other half: "And I will give peace in the land, and you shall lie down and none shall make you afraid" (Lev. 26:6). That accounts, also, for the logic of intelligible discourse that served that system so well.

The satisfying sense of composition, proportion, and order conveyed by the pentateuchal system finds no counterpart afterward, as we shall now see. No other Judaic system would remotely succeed as did the pentateuchal system in its systemic cogency, in its completeness and order, in its sense of the correspondence of ethos to ethics, in its power to generate a logic fitting to the systemic statement. The Jewish intellect began at its pinnacle of success. No wonder that, to the rightly pleased authorship of the pentateuchal Judaism, viewing the results of their handiwork, a sufficient pseudepigraphic attribution for aesthetic, not only political, reasons, could be only to God on high, through Moses as mere tradent. The modesty of situating themselves merely as last and least in a line of tradition was systemically beyond imagining. Such forthright pride in their achievement in system-buidling from a secular angle of vision is entirely justified. For, from the the system-builders' perspective on what they had made, as a matter of simple fact only God could have wrought it. No Judaic system-builders ever disagreed with them, though all would tacitly reject their system as it came forth by rereading, each authorship in its terms, what had come forth as a closed and completed system, that is to say, "from Sinai."

Part Two

THE POLITICAL ECONOMY OF JUDAISM

Chapter Four

One Goal of Systemic Analysis:
Toward the Political Economy of Religion
A Programmatic Statement

I propose to undertake the development of the field of the political economy of religion, exemplified through the case of Judaism in its classical age. Political economy joins the study of the institutions of the management of power we know as the politics of a society with the analysis of the disposition of scarce resources we know as economics. In prior ages, the ideas that governed collective life and conduct, that is, political ideas, encompassed issues of material life generally deemed economic, and in the interstices and interplay of both politics and economics, large-scale conceptions of the public interest and of society took shape. Plato's *Republic* and Aristotle's *Politics*, particularly the latter, pay ample attention to economics in the setting of politics, and, in the case of Aristotle, what the system says about economics forms a chapter within the larger statement of the system as a whole.

And that is the point at which religion becomes a matter of acute interest. For religious systems may make statements not only about matters we identify as theology but also about economics and political behavior. Religions are today studied as modes of making social worlds, but that language very commonly veils considerable uncertainty about what we wish to know about the "making of a social world" that a religion proposes to accomplish (and may actually effect). In any event one universal criterion for the differentiation and classification of religious systems is whether or not a religious system addresses, encompasses within its system, the realm of political economy. Some do, some don't. Christianity in late antiquity had virtually nothing to say about economics and cannot be said to have affected political economy at all, while in medieval times, with its encounter with Aristotle in particular, Christianity in the West worked out a political economy that predominated until the eighteenth century, when politics went its way, and economics became disembedded from the political world. It is perfectly self-evident that, from antiquity, Judaism, and from its beginning in early medieval times, Islam, have taken as critical the issues of political economy and have assumed a powerful role in the organization of politics and the management of economics. And other religious systems do as well. That is why the political economy of religions, how it is to be described, analyzed, and interpreted, forms a central concern for anyone interested in how humanity in the past, and the world today, sort out the issues of public policy for politics and economics alike.

Not only so, but until World War I, considerable interest attached to generalizations about political economy of religion. The field does not have to be invented, only renewed and reworked in light of things we have learned about religion and about the academic study of religion. For one major example, Weber's *Protestant Ethic and the Spirit of Capitalism* was only a chapter in public discussion, alongside Sombart's work on the theory that capitalism arose not from the Protestants but from the Jews. Weber, as you recall, worked on China, India, and ancient Israel as well, asking about the relationships between religious belief and the conduct of political economy, that is, rational economic action within a defined political framework of power relationships, all read against the backdrop of beliefs about "the sacred" or other religious concerns. So we may say that the political economy of religions is an old subject. But it has to be reworked, since we now realize that belief-systems of religion form only one part of the whole, and not, as even Weber posited, the centerpiece of interest. Since Weber we have learned much about religion and how to study religion, but we have not pursued Weber's questions. And that is why, through the reengagement with political economy as a dimension of religious systems and their construction of societies and world views, I propose to renew a discipline that, well over half a century ago, had already proved its worth in helping us to understand not merely religions, but religion, as the formative force in human civilization.

But political economy of religion assuredly requires renewal, and available work guides only as to goal, but not as to method, and that is for two reasons. First, because none of the inherited work accomplished the useful description of the religions under study. The ways in which religions were described have vastly changed. My work on systemic description, analysis, and interpretation of religions, focused on Judaism, shows in the contrast with Weber's *Ancient Judaism* that we have made many steps forward since that time, and it has rendered utterly obsolete every word in Weber's book. Second, because, in point of fact, while the issues of political economy in relationship to religion retain their urgency, in Islam, Christendom, and the worlds of India and Southeast Asia, for example, so that we cannot speak of Latin America without its Liberation Theology, a vast statement upon issues of political economy, systematic and critical work is virtually unknown. In the range of theory and accurate description, analysis, and interpretation of the political economy of a religious world, and in the comparison of the political economy of one religious system with that of another, so far as I know, scholarship in the study of religion has fallen silent. And yet, as we now recognize, there is simply no coping with the world today without the intellectual tools for understanding religion, not as a theory of another world, but as a power and force in the shaping of this world. Events in Iran and Afghanistan, as to Islam, Latin America and Poland, as to Roman Catholic Christianity, the State of Israel and the USA, as to Judaism, only illustrate that simple fact that most (though not all) of humanity does what it does by reason of religious conviction. And since public policy falls silent before that fact, it is time to reenter discourse with issues long dormant on the relationship between religious systems and the world of politics and of economics.

But in universities, this is done in a way particular to scholarship, in full recognition that, beyond universities, what we learn will be put to good use by others in the framing of public policy, a partnership of learning. What we do is address not concrete and practical issues of the other, but matters of theory that may guide those who do make policy. The bureaucracy of course depends upon research done on contract, and that involves not merely collecting and analyzing facts, but gaining a long perspective and working out a useful theory that will guide staff in collecting and analyzing facts and so working out the everyday policy that the bureaucracy effects. What we require is hypotheses and the testing of hypotheses against facts, and hypotheses emerge, to begin with, in the trial and error of particular cases: asking questions, attempting answers, testing hypotheses, explaining things. So long as a case is meant to exemplify, so long as we ask of a case, why this, not that? with a sustained answer meant to generate a theory, the case is not the mere collecting and arranging of facts but an exercise in description, analysis, and interpretation.

Now to the case of the political economy of religion and the way in which I propose to bring that area of learning to a new birth. I use as my case the Judaism of late antiquity, because that is one religious system that did, indeed, develop a large-scale conception of political economy, that is to say, that is a religious system that made its encompassing statement, also, through what it had to say about the household as the irreducible unit of production, about the market and its role in rationing scarce goods, and about wealth and its relationship to money (and to land, as a matter of fact). In this regard, that Judaism carried forward in a way, so far as I know unique in ancient times the systematic thought of Aristotle, the only figure in antiquity who had anything important to say about economics. The system of that Judaism, further, paid ample attention also to the disposition of issues and institutions of power we know as political science, once again, a remarkable labor of large-scale social thought. The study, therefore, of the political economy of ancient Judaism, beginning in the law codes and other writings of that Judaism, seems to me a promising area in which to develop the intellectual tools – points of inquiry, modes of thought – that will serve as a useful model in studying the political economy of Islam, in its varieties and rich diversity, as well as of Christianities of medieval and modern times. It goes without saying that the reading of the law for other than legal theory, so far as the study of antiquity is concerned, also is not a commonplace inquiry.

My own preparation for this work began with my study of the logical structures of the writings of ancient Judaism, yielding first *The Economics of Judaism. The Initial Statement.* Then came, in succession, *The Making of the Mind of Judaism. The Classical Age,* and, second, *The Formation of the Jewish Intellect. Making Connections and Drawing Conclusions in the Traditional System of Judaism.* Reading for this work and conversations with colleagues here have broadened my conception and made me realize that Aristotle is the model for this system as a whole, combining as he did the issues of the material sustenance of society and the political organization of society, and, of course, exercising a sustaining influence nearly down to the eighteenth century Physiocrats, founders of economics as we now know it.

It was with my study of Plato and Aristotle in the setting of economics, as I looked for the affinities and influences on the thought of the writers of the formative documents of Judaism, that my notion of the "re-founding" of political economy of religion as a subfield of the academic study of religion came up. The three essays that follow set forth some of the initial findings in this work on political economy in the instance of Judaism. Among them, the next covers ground not treated in my *Economics of Judaism* at all, and the next two are revised and abbreviated statements, for colleagues unlikely to work their way through the fully documented work, of some of the salient findings.

Chapter Five

The Political Economy of Judaism:
A Preliminary Definition of What Is At Stake

[Aristotle] will be seen as attacking the problem of man's livelihood with a radicalism of which no later writer on the subject was capable – none has ever penetrated deeper ito the material organization of man's life. In effect, he posed, in all its breadth, the question of the place occupied by the economy in society.

Karl Polanyi[1]

Economics from Aristotle to Quesnay and Riqueti, in the eighteenth century, dealt with not the science of wealth but rather "the management of the social household, first the city, then the state."[2] Economics disembedded from politics developed only in the eighteenth century. Prior to that time, it formed a principal part of the study of political economy. That is to say, economics formed a component of the larger sociopolitical order and dealt with the organization and management of the household *(oikos)*. The city *(polis)* was conceived as comprising a set of households. Political economy, therefore, presented the theory of the construction of society, the village, town, or city, out of households, a neat and orderly, intensely classical and, of course, utterly fictive conception. One part of that larger political economy confronted issues of the household and its definition as the principal unit of economic production, the market and its function within the larger political structure, and the nature and definition of wealth. In political economics of Judaism, we deal in particular with the economic part of the encompassing social thought of the initial statement of the Judaism of the dual Torah.[3] To begin with, we must recognize, beginning to end, that that thought forms part of the larger theory of the life and

---

[1] "Aristotle Discovers the Economy," in Polanyi et al., eds., *Trade and Market in the Early Empires*, p. 66.

[2] Elizabeth Fox-Genovese, *The Origins of Physiocracy. Economic Revolution and Social Order in Eighteenth-Century France* (Ithaca and London: Cornell University Press), p. 9. See also Karl Polanyi, *The Lifelihood of Man.* Edited by Harry W. Pearson (N.Y., San Francisco, and London: Academic Press, 1977), p. 7.

[3] Self-evidently, in future work, I shall come to the politics of Judaism in that same initial statement.

social existence of "Israel," as the theorists represented by the Mishnah understood that social entity in its political and economic existence in the here and now and also in the model of Heaven. What I mean, therefore, by political economy is the study of how a given religious system makes its overriding statement through its judgments of politics and economics, as much as through theology, myth, ritual, and philosophy.

My proposed mode of analysis therefore treats not the issues of economics broadly construed as (mere) economics, e.g., how the framers of the Mishnah understood the difference between a commodity and specie, or how they defined the fundamental unit of production. Nor do I suggest that we ask about facts of economic history at a given point in the history of a religious group, in the case at hand, for instance, about the economy of the Jews in the time of the Mishnah or how the Mishnah reveals economic information or even attitudes. What I want to know is the answer to a different question. It is, specifically, what we learn about a religion, e.g., the Judaism of the dual Torah in its initial statement when we ask those questions that economics instructs us to ask. So the issue is systemic analysis: I invoke economics as an indicator (and, I would claim, an independent variable) of the character of a system in context. From economics as conceived in antiquity, for instance, we gain perspective on the way in which the framers of the Mishnah appealed, also, to economics in stating their world view and way of life.

What the present perspective teaches is that the Mishnah is a document of political economy, in which the two critical classifications are the village, *polis*, and the household, *oikos*. Since, however, the Mishnah's framers conceived of the world as God's possession and handiwork, theirs was the design of a universe in which God's and humanity's realms flowed together. The result is a distributive economics, familiar from most ancient times onward, but a distributive economics that, in the same system, coexisted with a kind of market economics.[4] The Mishnah's statement bears comparison, therefore, to Plato's *Republic* and Aristotle's *Politics* as a utopian program *(Staatsroman)* of a society as a political entity, encompassing, also, its economics; but pertinent to the comparison also is Augustine's conception of a city of God and a city of man. In the Mishnah we find thinkers attempting, in acute detail, to think through how God and humanity form a single *polis* and a single *oikos*, a shared political economy, one village and one household on earth as it is in heaven.[5]

---

[4]I explain this matter in my *Economics of Judaism. The Initial Statement* (in press).
[5]That is why I conceive the more profound inquiry to address the politics of Judaism, as the Mishnah presents that politics: the city of God which is the city of humanity, unlike the distinct cities conceived by Augustine. The matter is neatly expressed in numerous specific rules. See for example Roger Brooks, *Support for the Poor in the Mishnaic Law of Agriculture: Tractate Peah* (Chico, California: Scholars Press for Brown Judaic Studies, 1983), p. 49 to Mishnah-

The Mishnah's sages placed economics, both market (for civil transactions) and distributive (for sacred transactions, e.g., with scheduled castes and the temple), in the center of their system, devoting two of their six divisions to it (the first and the fourth, for the distributive and the market economics, respectively), and succeeded in making their statement through economics in a sustained and detailed way far beyond the manner in which Aristotle did. And no one in antiquity came near Aristotle, as I said. It was with remarkable success that the sages of Judaism presented an economics wholly coordinated in a systemic way with a politics. In this proposed kind of study of religion and economics, therefore, we find ourselves on the border between sociology and economics, following how the sociology of economics – and therefore this kind of inquiry concerning religious materials places us squarely into the middle of discourse on political economy. Compared to the work of Plato and Aristotle, the Mishnah's system presents the single most successful political economy accomplished in antiquity.

What about work on the political economy of Judaism that is already in hand? The economics of Judaism, as the economics of the Jews, is hardly an unexplored field of inquiry.[6] Indeed, any study of pertinent topics, whether of the Jews' economics or of the Jews' own economy, of the Jews in economic life or of the economics of Judaism, takes its place in a long, if somewhat irregular and uneven, line of works on the subject. The most important and best known statement on the economics of Judaism purports to account, by appeal to the economics of Judaism and the economic behavior of Jews, for the origins of

---

tractate Peah 1:4-5: "The Mishnah's framers regard the Land as the exclusive property of God. When Israelite farmers claim it as their own and grow food on it, they must pay for using God's earth. Householders thus must leave a portion of the yield unharvested as *peah* and give this food over to God's chosen representatives, the poor. The underlying theory is that householders are tenant farmers who pay taxes to their landlord, God." In this concrete way the interpenetration of the realms of God and humanity is expressed. That conception of the household and the village made up of households, the *oikos* and the *polis,* yields not only an economics, such as we treat here in Chapters Five through Seven and Eight, but also a politics. And the politics is the foundation for the economics, as we shall repeatedly observe.

[6]For an introduction to the economic study of talmudic literature, see Roman A. Ohrenstein, "Economic Thought in Talmudic Literature in the Light of Modern Economics," *The American Journal of Economics and Sociology* 1968, 27:185-96, who cites earlier writings on the subject, cf. p. 185, n. 3. Later in this article we shall deal with some of the work that has been done. Ohrenstein's "Economic Self-Interest and Social Progress in Talmudic Literature: A Further Study of Ancient Economic Thought and its Modern Significance," *American Journal of Economics and Sociology* 1970, 29:59-70, typifies the work in hand in that field. I do not here treat Tamari's work on Jewish ethics vis-à-vis economics, because that seems to me a methodologically still more primitive work than any under discussion here.

modern capitalism. Werner Sombart, *The Jews and Modern Capitalism*,[7] in 1911 set the issues of the economics of Judaism within a racist framework, maintaining that Jews exhibited an aptitude for modern capitalism, and that aptitude derives in part from the Jewish religion, in part from the Jews' national characteristics. Jewish intellectuality, teleological mode of thought, energy, mobility, adaptability, Jews' affinity for liberalism and capitalism, – all of these accounted for the role of Jews in the creation of the economics of capitalism, which dominated. Sombart appealed, in particular, to the anthropology of the Jew, maintaining that the Jews comprise a distinct anthropological group. Jewish qualities persist throughout their history: "constancy in the attitude of the Jews to the peoples among whom they dwelt, hatred of the Jews, Jewish elasticity." "The economic activities of the Jew also show a remarkable constancy." Sombart even found the knowledge of economics among the rabbis of the Talmud to be remarkable. In the end Sombart appealed to the fact that the Jews constitute a "Southern people transplanted among Northern peoples." The Jews exhibited a nomadic spirit through their history. Sombart contrasted "the cold North and the warm South," and held that "Jewish characteristics are due to a peculiar environment." So he appealed to what he found to be the correlation between Jewish intellectuality and desert life, Jewish adaptability and nomad life, and wrote about "Jewish energy and their Southern origin," "'Sylvanism' and Feudalism compared with 'Saharaism' and Capitalism," and ended, of course, with the theme of the Jews and money and the Jews and the Ghetto.

The romantic and racist view of the Jews as a single continuing people with innate characteristics which scientific scholarship can identify and explain of course formed the premise for Sombart's particular interest, in the economic characteristics of the Jew and the relationship of this racial traits to the Jews' origin in the desert. While thoroughly discredited, these views have nonetheless generated a long sequence of books on Jews' economic behavior. Today people continue to conceive "Jewish economic history" as a cogent subject that follows not only synchronic and determinate, but also diachronic and indeterminate lines and dimensions. Such books have taken and now take as the generative category the Jews' constituting a distinct economy, or their formation of a social unit of internally consistent economic action and therefore thought, the possibility of describing, analyzing, and interpreting the Jews within the science of economics. But that category and its premise themselves still await definition and demonstration, and these to this day are yet lacking. Consequently, while a considerable literature on "the Jews' economic history" takes for granted that there is a single, economically cogent group, the Jews, which has had a single ("an") economic history, and which, therefore, forms a distinctive unit of

---

[7]The edition I consulted is Werner Sombart, *The Jews and Modern Capitalism*. With a new introduction by Samuel Z. Klausner. Translated by M. Epstein (New Brunswick and London: Transaction Books, 1982).

economic action and thought, the foundations for that literature remain somewhat infirm.[8]

The conception of Jews' having an economic history, part of the larger, indeed encompassing, notion of the Jews' having had a single history as a people, one people, has outlived the demise of the racist rendition of the matter by Sombart. But what happens when we take seriously the problems of conception and method that render fictive and merely imposed a diachronic history of the Jews, unitary, harmonious, and continuous? And what happens when we realize that the secondary and derivative conception of a diachronic economics of the Jews is equally dubious? Whether or not it is racist, that unitary conception of the Jews as a single, distinctive, ongoing historical entity, a social group forming also a cogent unit of economic action, is surely romantic. Whatever the salubrious ideological consequences, such an economics bypasses every fundamental question of definition and method. If the Jews do not form a distinct economy, then how can we speak of the Jews in particular in an account of economic history? If, moreover, the Jews do not form a distinct component of a larger economy, then what do we learn about economics when we know that (some) Jews do this, others, that? And if Jews, in a given place and circumstance, constitute a distinct economic unit within a larger economy, then how study Jews' economic action out of the larger economic context which they help define and of which they form a component? The upshot of these question is simple: how shall we address those questions concerning rational action with regard to scarcity that do, after all, draw our attention when we contemplate, among other entities, the social entities that Jews have formed, and now form, in the world?

True, the simple fact that Jews have lived in a variety of political and economic settings has not escaped attention. The further fact that Jews' economies flourish within larger economies, on the one hand, and do not form a single continuum through time, on the other, has found recognition. But these obstacles to describing "Jewish economic history" have not prevented the composition of pictures of Jews' economics and Judaism's economics. One solution is simple. People assemble pictures of traits held to have proved common to Jews in whatever circumstances in which they conduct their economic activities. These are adduced in justification of the description not merely of diverse Jews' economic action, but of "*the* Jews' economic history." The appeal is to a principal distinctive trait, allegedly indicative of Jews and not

---

[8]I hasten to state at the outset that Jews' role in diverse economies, so far as that role is distinctive, surely permits us to appeal as an independent variable to the fact that certain economic actors are Jews. But what trait or quality about those actors as Jews explains the distinctive traits of Jews as a group – if any does – requires careful analysis in a comparative framework, e.g., Jews as a distinct component of a variety of economies. None of these entirely valid and intellectually rigorous inquires is under discussion here.

of others and therefore demonstrative of Jews' forming an economic entity, namely, Jews' "marginality." Whether or not that characterization has received precise definition need not detain us. The impressionistic character of the category, its relative and subjective applicability – these matters need not detain us.

But let us grant for the moment that "economic marginality" forms a category subject to investigation and replication. Then we surely notice that other groups have taken a marginal place in society and economics as well. Accordingly, the possibility that Jews' economic action and thought exemplifies not their "Jewish" and so their ideological traits but their (allegedly) marginal character has not yet attracted attention.[9] It follows that while some may claim to present the Jews as an example of any "marginal" economic unit, without differentiating the case from the law of marginal economic action in general, others, and they form the larger part of the literature, do not even take the trouble.

But the picture of how such subjects as "Jews in economic life," and "economic history of the Jews" – both titles of books, cited presently – are treated is hardly complete with these abstract observations. Let me point to how the work has actually been done. This I do in two steps, first dealing with work I believe entirely sound and correct on Jews' economic behavior, then with another, and more common, reading of the topic, a conceptually crude and incompetent one. Studies of Jews as an economic entity or of Jews' economic behavior include work that speaks not of all Jews everywhere and at all times, in the manner of Sombart, but of a particular subset of Jews, in a distinct economic, therefore also political-historical, setting. Such responsible scholarship establishes as fact, rather than treating as premise, that Jews did form a subset of an economy and did constitute an economic unit. Such entirely correct economics of Jews further examines Jews' economic behavior not as an effect of ideology but as entirely rational within the public rationality of economic action in the face of scarcity. And, finally, such work deals with Jews who as a matter of public policy were treated as a distinct economic unit and subjected to rules applicable only to that one unit, ample justification for studying the Jews' economy as a distinct subset of the larger economy at hand. I point as a model of work on Jews' economic history to Arcadius Kahan, *Essays in Jewish Social and Economic History*.[10] Specific to a particular economy, concerned with showing that the Jews formed a distinct economic actor within

---

[9]We may ignore the flip and indefensible racism in such odd comparisons as yield the statement, "The overseas Chinese are the Jews of the Orient," and the like. These form no exception to the judgment that the comparative study of supposedly marginal economic entities awaits systematic attention, at least in writing about the Jews.

[10]Edited by Roger Weiss, with an introduction by Jonathan Frankel. Chicago and London: The University of Chicago Press, 1986.

that economy, Kahan's papers seem to me the model for how economic history is to be done on this subject. As to allegations that ideology intervenes in economic action and therefore explains it, applied to the Jews in the notion that "Judaism" leads to economic action of one sort rather than another, in such wise that, in the absence of that "Judaism," Jews would have acted like everyone else, Kahan's papers prove indifferent.[11] It may prove to be a fact that a Judaism shapes not only attitudes but actions, not only in religion but also in economics. But until proven for a given circumstance, that is not a fact; and unless proven for all contexts, it surely cannot explain Jews' economic behavior.

But Kahan's essay does not form the paramount model of "Jewish economic history," rather, it defines the exception to the rule. Contrasting to Kahan's formulation of a precise area of study and investigation of that area through ample data are several works exemplary of inappropriate readings of the matter. These works are characterized by faults of method, conception, and execution. As to method, they impute to all Jews everywhere traits demonstrated in a single case. As to conception, they take for granted that sayings attributed to authorities by texts composed long after said authorities lived actually were said by those authorities, and, further, that people did precisely what sages said they should do. As to execution, they display considerable difficulty in composing cogent paragraphs and well-crafted arguments. In all, a work on the economics of Judaism, not on Jews' economic behavior or on an alleged correlation between the economics of Judaism and Jews' economic behavior or economics or formation of economies, does well to review how these subjects have been handled even by substantial figures of our own time.

One representative example is Salo W. Baron,[12] who claims to know about economic trends among Jews in the second, third, and fourth centuries. As evidence he cites episodic statements of rabbis, as in the following:

> In those days R. Simon ben Laqish coined that portentous homily which, for generations after, was to be quoted in endless variations: "'You shall not cut yourselves,' this means you shall not divide yourselves into separate groups ...." Before the battle for ethnic-religious survival, the inner class struggle receded.

> Age-old antagonisms, to be sure, did not disappear overnight. The conflict between the scholarly class and "the people of the land" continued for several generations.

---

[11]I refer in particular to "The Impact of Industrialization in Tsarist Russia on the Socioeconomic Conditions of the Jewish Population," in Kahan, *op. cit.*, pp. 1-69.

[12]*A Social and Religious History of the Jews* (New York: Columbia University Press, 1952) II. *Ancient Times,* Part II, pp. 241-260. Compare my "Why No Science in Judaism?" in *From Description to Conviction* (Atlanta: Scholars Press for Brown Judaic Studies, 1987), on the counterpart problems of intellect exhibited by Saul Lieberman, Baron's contemporary.

> Class differences as such likewise receded into the background as the extremes of wealth and poverty were leveled down by the unrelenting pressure of Roman exploitation. Rarely do we now hear descriptions of such reckless display of wealth as characterized the generation of Martha, daughter of Boethos, before the fall of Jerusalem. Even the consciously exaggerated reports of the wealth of the patriarchal house in the days of Judah I fell far short of what we know about the conspicuous consumption of the Herodian court and aristocracy.[13]

It would be difficult to find a better example of overinterpretation of evidence – to begin with, irrelevant to the point – than Baron's concluding sentence of the opening paragraph of this abstract. Not having shown that there was an inner class struggle or even spelled out what he means by class struggle, not having shown how he knows the category applies, let alone the evidence for social stratification on which such judgments rest, Baron leaps into his explanation for why the class struggle receded. That is not the only evidence of what can only be regarded as indifference to critical issues characteristic of writing on Jews' economies, but it is probative. The rest of the passage shows how on the basis of no sustained argument whatsoever, Baron invokes a variety of categories of economic history and analysis of his time, e.g., conspicuous consumption, class struggle ("inner" presumably different from "outer"), and on and on.

When discussing economic policies, which draw us closer to the subject of this book, Baron presents a discussion some may deem fatuous.[14] Precisely how he frames the issues of economic theory will show why: "Economic Policies: Here too we may observe the tremendous influence of talmudic legislation upon Jewish economy." The premise that there was (a) Jewish economy, and that talmudic legislation affected economic action, is simply unsubstantiated. How Baron knows that people did what rabbis said they should, or that Jews formed an economy in which people could make decisions in accord with sages' instructions, he does not say. The premise of all that follows, then, is vacant. More to the point of our interest in matters of economic theory, we turn to Baron's program of discourse on what he has called "policies:"

> The rabbis constantly tried to maintain interclass equilibrium. They did not denounce riches, as some early Christians did, but they emphasized the merely relative value of great fortune fortunes .... The persistent accentuation of collective economic responsibility made the Jewish system of public welfare highly effective. While there was much poverty among the Jews, the community, through its numerous charitable institutions, took more or less adequate care of the needy.

---

[13]Baron, p. 241.
[14]Baron, pp. 251-255.

Man's right, as well as duty, to earn a living and his freedom of disposing of property were safeguarded by rabbinic law and ethics only in so far as they did not conflict with the common weal ....

Private ownership, too, was hedged with many legal restrictions and moral injunctions in favor of over-all communal control ....

Rabbinic law also extended unusual protection to neighbors ....

Nor did the individual enjoy complete mastery over testamentary dispositions ....

Apart from favoring discriminatory treatment of apostates, who were supposed to be dead to their families, the rabbis evinced great concern for the claims of minor children to support from their fathers' estate ....

In a period of economic scarcity social interest demanded also communal control over wasteful practices even with one's own possessions.

How this mélange of this and that – something akin to economic policy, some odd observations on public priority over private interest that sounds suspiciously contemporary (to 1952), counsel about not throwing away bread crumbs – adds up to "economic policies" I cannot say. But the data deserves a still closer scrutiny, since Baron represents the state of economic analysis of Judaism and so exemplifies precisely the problem I propose to solve in a different way. Here is his "man's right" paragraph:

Man's right, as well as duty, to earn a living and his freedom of disposing of property were safeguarded by rabbinic law and ethics only in so far as they did not conflict with the common weal. Extremists like R. Simon ben Yohai insisted that the biblical injunction, "This book of the law shall not depart out of thy mouth, but thou shalt meditate therein day and night," postulated wholehearted devotion to the study of Torah at the expense of all economic endeavors. But R. Ishmael effectively countered by quoting the equally scriptural blessing, "That thou mayest gather in thy corn and thy wine and thine oil." Two centuries later, the Babylonian Abbaye, who had started as a poor man and through hard labor and night work in the fields had amassed some wealth, observed tersely, "Many have followed the way of R. Ishmael and succeeded; others did as R. Simeon ben Yohai and failed." Sheer romanticism induced their compeer, R. Judah bar Ila'i, to contend that in olden times people had made the study of the law a full-time occupation, and devoted only little effort to earning a living, and hence had proved successful in both .... R. Simeon ben Yohai himself conceded, however, that day and night meditation had been possible only to a generation living on Mannah or to priestly recipients of heave-offerings .... In practice the rabbis could at best secure, as we shall see, certain economic privileges for a minority of students, relying upon the overwhelming majority of the population to supply society's needs to economically productive work.

From the right to earn a living being limited by the common weal, we jump to study of the Torah as the alternative to productive labor. That move of Baron's I cannot myself claim to interpret. I see no connection between the balance between "freedom of disposing of property" and "conflict with the common weal," on the one side, and "the issue of work as against study, on the other. The rest of the discussion concerns only that latter matter, and the paragraph falls to pieces by the end in a sequence of unconnected sayings joined by a pseudo-narrative ("two centuries later") and an equally meretricious pretense of sustained argument "himself conceded"), all resting on the belief that the sayings assigned to various sages really were said by them.

This reading by Baron of how "the Jews'" policies and behavior in economics are to be studied should not be set aside as idiosyncratic. The obvious flaws of historical method, the clear limitations in even so simple a matter as the competent construction of a paragraph – these should not obscure the fact that Baron's construction of the Jewish economy and Jewish economic policy is representative and not at all idiosyncratic. The received conception first of all imputes to the Jews a single economic history, which can be traced diachronically. Proof lies in works in both English and Hebrew. Take for example the book entitled, *Economic History of the Jews*, assigned to Salo W. Baron, Arcadius Kahan, and others, edited by Nachum Gross.[15] Baron wrote Chapters One through Seven, Kahan, Eight through Ten, of Part One, "general survey," and the titles of these sequential chapters follow: "the first temple period, exile and restoration, the second temple period, the talmudic era, the Muslim Middle Ages, medieval Christendom, economic doctrines, the early modern period, the transition period, the modern period." That, I contend, is a program of diachronic economic history. These chapters can have been composed and presented in the sequence before us only if the author assumed that a single group, with a continuous, linear history, formed also a cogent and distinct economic entity, with its own, continuous, linear, economic history.

"Economic doctrines" as Baron expounds them are amply familiar to us: bits and pieces of this and that. The remainder of the book covers these topics: agriculture, industry, services, and each part is subdivided, e.g., under services: "banking and bankers, brokers, contractors, court Jews, department stores, Jewish autonomous finances, market days and fairs, mintmasters and moneyers, moneylending, peddling, secondhand goods, slave trade, spice trade, stock exchanges." Here again, we may be sure, data on department stores derive from one time and place, those on slave trade, from another. But laid forth sequentially, the chapter titles indicate a conception of a single unitary and continuous economic history, in which any fact concerning any Jew at any time or place connects with any fact concerning any other Jew at any other time or place, the whole forming a cogent economy. Nor should work in Hebrew be expected to exhibit a more critical definition of what is subject to discourse. The same Nachum Gross edited *Jews in Economic Life. Collected Essays In*

---

[15]New York: Schocken, 1975.

Memory of Arkadius Kahan (1920-1982).[16] Here is the portrait of a field, as sequential essays outline that field:

The Economic Activities of the Jews

The Cardinal Elements of the Economy of Palestine during the Herodian Period

The Economy of Jewish Communities in the Golan in the Mishnah and Talmud Period

The Itinerant Peddler in Roman Palestine

The German Economy in the 13th-14th Centuries

The Framework and Conditions for the Economic Activity of the Jews

On the Participation of Jewish Businessmen in the Production and Marketing of Salt in Sixteenth Century Poland and Lithuania

Economic Activities of Jews in the Caribbean in Colonial Times

Jewish Guilds in Turkey in the Sixteenth to Nienteenth Centuries

and on and on. Nor do I exaggerate the utter confusion generated by the conception of "the Jews" as an economic entity, continuous from beginning to the present. The juxtaposition of these two papers seems to me to make the point rather sharply:

Jewish Population and Occupations in Sherifian Morocco

On the Economic Activities of the Moldavian Jews in the Second Half of the 18th and the First Half of the 19th centuries

There is no need to ask what one thing has to do with the other. We just take for granted that Jews are Jews wherever they lived, whenever they thrived, and whatever Jews' occupations were in Sherifian Morocco bears a self-evident relationship to whatever Moldavian Jews did for a living half a world and a whole civilization distant. Having cited the juxtaposition of titles, with justified confidence I simply rest my case.

How then do I propose to proceed? First, let me make explicit what I do not believe forms a valid program of inquiry in economic history. I reject as hopelessly obtuse the diachronic study of what Jews in various times and places have done to make a living, that is, Jews' economies, or Jews' roles in economies. We should have to demonstrate that, on their own, Jews constituted autonomous economic units, for such studies to yield consequential hypotheses.

---

[16]Jerusalem: The Zalman Shazar Center for the Furtherance of the Study of Jewish History, 1985.

Whether or not at specific points Jews formed cogent economic units, whether or not at other points Jews formed cogent components of economies made up of diverse other ethnic components, whether or not indicative traits of an ethnic character have any bearing at all upon economic analysis, whether or not ideological elements of indicative traits of an ethnic character constitute independent variables in economic action – none of these questions seems to me properly framed when its comes to "the Jews."

If treating "the Jews" as a social and economic entity yields utter confusion, recognizing that, at a given time and place, in a given set of writings, a cogent statement of a Judaic system, consisting of a world view, a way of life, addressed to a distinct and defined social group, an "Israel," did reach expression, this permits analysis of another sort. It is inquiry into the economic thought of a Judaism. Let me briefly set forth the kind of inquiry that, I believe, will contribute to our understanding of the history of economic theory within the setting, also, of Judaism.

Economics forms a critical component of a system of thought intended to design and to describe a social world. No utopian design, such as is given by the Mishnah, a classic *Staatsroman* or political novel in the tradition of Plato's *Republic* and Aristotle's *Politics*, can ignore the material organization of society, and every important system of a social character encompasses issues of the social doctrine for economic life. True, in modern times we are accustomed to view economics as disembedded from the political and social system, the market, for instance, as unrelated to kinship or institutions of culture. But until the eighteenth century, by contrast, economics was understood as a component of the social system, and also a constituent of the cultural context. It follows that those religious systems that propose to prescribe public policy and design a social world will integrate into their systems theories of economic behavior and also accounts of systemically correct economic policy. But how does a religion make its statement, also, through its economics? That is the question I believe we should answer when we consider the economic theory of a religion.

The Mishnah, the initial statement of the Judaism of the dual Torah, ca. A.D. 200, not only encompasses but also integrates economics within its larger system and makes its statement, also, through the exquisite details of rules and regulations governing the householder, the market, and wealth. In this regard, the authorship of the Mishnah finds a comfortable place within the age in which the Mishnah was framed. For its remarkably successful capacity to make its systemic statement, also, through the concerns of economics, its capacity to accomplish the detailed exegesis of economics within its larger social vision and system – these lack a significant counterpart in the generality of philosophy and theology in ancient times. In theologies of Christianity, for one example, we find slight interest in, or use of, theories on the household, markets, and wealth, in the framing of the Christian statement, which bears no judgment that we may identify as a statement upon, or of, political economy. Only when we turn to

Aristotle do we find a counterpart to the accomplishment of the authorship of the Mishnah. Indeed, as the Mishnah's authorship's power of the extraordinarily detailed exegesis of economics as a systemic component becomes clear to us, we shall conclude that, among the social theorists of antiquity, the framers of the Mishnah take first place in the sophistication and profundity of their thought within political economy.

Clearly, we must read in the context of thought on economics within the philosophy of the age the economics of Judaism in its initial statement, and that approach to the subject brings us to the single influential figure in economy theory, Aristotle. The power of economics as framed by Aristotle, the only economic theorist of antiquity worthy of the name, was to develop the relationship between the economy to society as a whole[17] And the framers of the Mishnah did precisely that: they incorporated issues of economics, even at a profound theoretical level, into the system of society as a whole, as they proposed to construct society. To paraphrase Polanyi's judgment of Aristotle, the authorship of the Mishnah is to be seen as attacking the problem of man's livelihood within a system of sanctification of a holy people with a radicalism of which no later religious thinkers about utopias were capable. None has ever penetrated deeper into the material organization of man's life under the aspect of God's rule. In effect, they posed, in all its breadth, the question of the critical, indeed definitive place occupied by the economy in society under God's rule.

In proposing the systemic analysis of economic thought within a larger religious context, I mean therefore to open many doors, but to close only one. It is the conception that, to define what "Judaism" (or Christianity, Islam, or some other religion) says about a subject, we merely collect and arrange and so compose into a neat collection defined by the topic at hand all topically pertinent sayings, from all times and places and documents, hence from all Judaisms and all groups of Jews. But that is very commonly how people proceed, that is, without regard to the always determinative dimension of context, let alone to inner logic and systemic discipline and setting. So they present dissertations on topics generally deemed to be, as in the present instance, those of economics. These dissertations may assemble little more than bits and pieces of uninterpreted data about Jews in the spice trade or in department stores, slave trade or diamonds, and brokerage or junk. But on that basis we know nothing at all about "Jewish economic history," the economics of "Judaism" (whatever in context that can mean), let alone about economic actions characteristic of Jews or normative for Jews – and the reasons therefor. Even rather glib judgments about Jews' economic "marginality" stand for premises scarcely accessible to rational analysis.

It follows that mere hunting and gathering form no model for learning, since even data of the hardest kind require a context or remain mere gibberish. Sayings

---

[17]Polanyi, "Aristotle Discovers the Economy," p. 79.

about the value of work, about agronomics, currency, commerce and the marketplace, correct management of labor – by themselves these too tell us nothing about economics as a theoretical construct and as a component of a still larger construction of a world, and they certainly do not inform us about what people actually did.   Only a systematic reading of such sayings in the encompassing context of a full statement on the theory of economics made by a given Judaism in its well-crafted sources and their well-composed and cogent statement supplies the correct setting in which these discrete and episodic sayings gain meaning and yield consequence.   Once we ask about economics, we have to discover what *in the system at hand* constituted an aspect of economics, subject to the definition of economics we now deem serviceable, but transcending what, in the system in which we live, within that definition we understand as economics.

In the simple approach I propose, we may learn something about the theory of economics in the system under analysis.[18]   We shall learn nothing about economic behavior of Jews, either as individuals or as a group, at any time in their history. Let me make a simple statement about why I do not treat matters of fact – actual economic action, for instance – but focus only upon matters of theory. I simply dismiss as merely primitive any notion that people did, or do, what holy books allege they did or should do. That idle nonsense cannot detain learning any longer. We know only what the holy books, beginning with the Mishnah, said, but not what people actually did and why they did it. So the economic history of Jews in antiquity is accessible only in bits and pieces insufficient to compose an account either of the economics of the Jews of the land of Israel or, all the more so, the economic theory that is palpable in the things they actually did.

It may be of interest to point to further inquiries ahead. Specifically, that the same critique of "Jewish ecnomic history" and "the economics of Judaism" is to be said concerning the "Jews' political behavior" and the politics of Judaism is obvious.   But at this time, in general, studies of the politics of Jews in relationship to Judaism present a still more abysmal picture than those on the economics of Judaism and economic action of Jews. Collections of sayings on topics deemed political are published even now as accounts of "Jewish political theory" or "the political theory of Judaism," or even as efforts to explain Jews' political conduct in the past and in the world today. I find stupefying the methodological crudity of these modes of discourse on issues of economics, politics, and philosophy, when it comes to the study of the Jews and of Judaisms. I therefore do not exaggerate the theoretical and methodological state of affairs in saying that my establishing a systemic context, on the one side, and

---

[18]Given the long history of the official, Christian economics, from medieval times forward, I am inclined to see in the proposed renewal of political economy of religion a considerable program indeed. And then there is Islam!

my effort to find out what, within a system, economics was or is, represent radically new approaches.

The world-construction, Judaism, encompasses all subjects addressing an entire nation and society, "Israel," whatever group of Jews in such a world-construction constitutes "Israel." And such a program of world-construction therefore by its nature involves three principal intellectual tasks of theoretical thought. These cover the construction's theoretical statement, as a system, of a theory of politics, economics, and learning. Western civilization, for instance, rests upon the politics of democracy, the economics of capitalism,[19] and the learning of science and technology. What of the Judaic system of the dual Torah? Can we identify its politics, economics, and its modes of philosophical thought and systematic inquiry that form the counterpart to philosophy, including natural philosophy? Answers to that question form the first step in an effort to describe the world-construction, Judaism, in any of its versions ("Judaisms"). Not only so, but even today, both in the State of Israel and elsewhere, important systems of thought claim to set forth (a) Judaism by which groups of Jews may compose and construct their societies, their cultures, their ways of life and world views – their Judaism. Any claim to address the contemporary world in the name of that Judaism must answer the questions that world-constructions must answer and do answer, and (it goes without saying) statements of the answer must adduce in evidence and argument and syllogism not merely discrete and episodic sayings on this and that ("work hard") but a whole and considered theory of matters ("work hard because God works hard").

There is a still more interesting reason for engaging in the study of the economics, politics, and modes of thought we know as philosophy of a given Judaism. In the interpretation of any religious system, such as the Judaism of the dual Torah, we have to compare what one system sets forth with what other systems present. If we are to interpret the Judaism of the dual Torah consequently, we have to undertake comparison with other modes – competing modes indeed! – of the formation of (a) civilization. These are not only or, today, mainly religious. So far, therefore, as we wish to make sense of one system, we require occasions for comparison with other systems, such as are presented by economics, politics, and modes of thought.[20] But if we are to compare system to system, we have to learn, also, how to compare economics to economics, political economy to political economy, even to know what component of a given system serves as the counterpart and corresponding component to the economics of another system, beginning, of course, with our own. This book addresses in a very particular framework the question of translating from one culture to another the theory of economics, that is, rational

---

[19]Of which, I think it is clear, socialism must be regarded as an epiphenomenon of transient consequence.

[20]I refer to my *The Making of the Mind of Judaism. The Formative Age.*

action in regard to scarcity, and, in a subsidiary sense, also to the increase and disposition of wealth. What I wish to know is how we may describe the economics of a world different from our own, and so, ultimately, penetrate into the meaning of rationality, encompassing rational action in matters of scarcity and also wealth, its increase and disposition, in a universe other than the familiar one of the secular West.

To do so, we cannot simply adopt and apply to an alien world that contemporary and commonplace theory of economics that for us describes and accounts for the rationality of economic action. That would tell us nothing about rational economic action in a world in which rationality bears different rules from the ones we know. Rather, we have to identify within that other world, different from our own, the things that to them fell into the category we know as economic. Specifically, we ask, what are the things they regarded as rational actions in rational action in regard to scarcity, and also to matters of wealth, its increase and disposition? And how did they uncover hypotheses of rationality in economic action and test them and translate them into rules of intelligent economic action? In this way we do not merely adopt, but we adapt the issues of economics by allowing for economic action to follow rules different from the ones we know, yet to accord with conceptions we nonetheless can claim to understand.

Specifically, when we can answer those questions, we know the economics of that other world, that is, we can translate economics from one world to the other. We are able to ask our questions about economics – theory of rational action in the face of scarcity and in the increase and disposition of wealth – and also discern and understand alien answers to those same questions: our rationality constructing the program of inquiry into their rationality concerning common issues, differently sorted out.

Chapter Six

Aristotle's Political Economics
and the Mishnah's:
The Matter of Wealth and Usury

As Schumpeter presents matter, Aristotle's theory of money regards money as principally a medium of exchange. In order to serve as a medium of exchange in markets of commodities, money itself must be one of those commodities: "It must be a thing that is useful and has exchange value independently of its monetary function ... a value that can be compared with other values."[1] Money is contingent, serves a function, bears no intrinsic worth, constitutes a mere medium of exchange, like any other commodity. It cannot form a definition of wealth. The authorship of the Mishnah of course concurred, seeing silver and gold as fundamentally commodities, subject to redefinition, under specified circumstances, also as specie – in that order. And that accounts, also, for the Mishnah's authorship's understanding of wealth, hence also, their treatment of usury as essentially profit, pure and simple.

To the framers of the Mishnah, wealth meant real estate, that alone. Barter to them as to Aristotle was the correct mode of natural exchange, trade was unnatural. Barter involves not the increase of wealth, which is (to Aristotle) contrary to nature, but only exchanges to accommodate the needs of households, which, by nature, cannot be wholly self-sufficient. Money serves as a substitute for items of barter. But money also is something people wish to accumulate on its own, and that is unnatural. Household management satisfies the needs of the household; wealth beyond those needs is meaningless, unnatural. Retail trade aims at the accumulation of coins through exchanges; there is no natural limit to the desire for money, corresponding to the natural limit to the desire for commodities. Money serves all sorts of purposes and can be hoarded. Money is not the same thing as wealth. People confuse the two, however, as Davisson and Harper summarize Aristotle's view:

> The cause of this confusion is that wrong-headed men believe that the purposes of household management may be served by seeking and increasing bodily pleasures. Since the enjoyment of bodily pleasures

---

[1]Joseph A. Schumpeter, *History of Economic Analysis*, pp. 62-3.

depends upon property, their aims become the unlimited acquisition of
property, including money. When this occurs, men try to change every
art into the art of getting riches, and consequently they transform the art
of household management into the art of retail trade. But this is an
unnatural perversion and the two should be distinguished. The profit
motive attaches not to wealth but to the accumulation of riches or coin
which is accomplished in a market distinct from the state and the
household.[2]

Along these same lines, the authorship of the Mishnah takes a remarkably
unsympathetic view of the holder of liquid capital. The one who traded in goods,
the merchant, the shopkeeper, especially, the holder of capital, moneylender and
factor alike, were persons subjected to close restriction. The (land-poor)
householder is represented always as the borrower. The lender is persistently
treated as outsider, watched and regulated. The authorship of the Mishnah never
represents the householder as lending money to another householder. It knows
much about factors, who provide to a householder capital in the form of animals,
to be tended, raised, and sold, with both parties sharing the profits.

The Mishnah's deepest interest in factoring contracts was that the farmer not
work for nothing or for less than he put into the arrangement; that would smack
of "usury," which, in context, stands only for making money on one's
investment of liquid capital or its equivalent in livestock.[3] The position of the
householder encompassed true value not only in the notion that a sixth of
deviation from true value involved fraud, but in the conception that the value of
seed and crops may vary, but capital will not. Lending money for investment is
not permitted to yield a profit for the capitalist. True value (in our sense) lies in
the land and produce, not in liquid capital. Seed in the ground yields a crop.
Money invested in maintaining the agricultural community from season to
season does not. The bias is against not only usury but interest, in favor not
only of regulating fraud but restricting honest traders.

The conception of wealth just now outlined comes to concrete expression in
Mishnah tractate Baba Mesia Chapter Five, which defines "usury," applying and
expanding the scriptural prohibition against it. The chapter discusses the matters
of interest and increase, in line with Lev. 25:35-6. That prohibition forms the
arena in which the framers of the Mishnah define their conception of wealth, its
identification with land and the produce of land; the exclusion, from the notion
of wealth, of (mere) money; the indifference to capital and investment; and the
other aspects of the profoundly Aristotelian economics characteristic of their
system. It is a long and subtle discussion. Let us turn to the exposition of the

[2]Davisson and Harper, *European Economic History*, Vol. I, p. 128.
[3]For a current account of the issue of usury, cf. Paul E. Gottfried, "The Western
Case against Usury," *Thought*, 1985, 60:89-98, and compare Benjamin Nelson,
The Idea of Usury. From Tribal Brotherhood to Universal Brotherhood (Chicago:
University of Chicago Press, 1969).

remarkable chapter on the subject, containing, as it does, whatever theory of wealth, expressed in concrete detail, that our authorship proposes to impart to the actualities of everyday trade and commerce.

The chapter opens with a distinction between interest and increase. The former is defined simply as repayment of five *denars* for a loan of a *sela*, which consists of four *denars,* or repayment of three *seahs* of what for a loan of two. The going rate of interest appears to have been 25 percent for a loan in cash, and 50 percent for a loan in kind. We do not know the length of time of the loan. Increase is a somewhat more subtle question. It involves payment for delivery, later on, of a commodity valued at the market price prevailing at the time of the agreement. The one who pays the money in advance thus profits, since prices are much lower at harvest-time than in advance. Trading in futures occupies much attention. The prohibition of interest is expanded with great care at Mishnah tractate Baba Mesia 5:2-6. The concern not to trade in futures or to gain increase through commodities is at Mishnah tractate Baba Mesia 5:7-10. The main point is to treat as prohibited interest diverse sorts of payments in kind in consideration of a loan. Mishnah tractate Baba Mesia 5:2 prohibits the debtor from renting out to the creditor a courtyard at no cost or at less than the prevailing rate. It does allow a deduction for payment of rent in advance – a very different matter. Mishnah tractate Baba Mesia 5:3 takes into account the possibility of a subterfuge in which, in exchange for what is in fact a loan, the creditor enjoys the usufruct of a field. This matter will require close attention.

This brings us to what is an essentially unrelated matter, but one that, within Aristotle's theory of money, belongs together with "usury." "Interest" and "usury" we shall now see really stand for nothing less than "profit," that is, *getting money not through barter.*[4] Mishnah tractate Baba Mesia 5:4 goes on to prohibit interest in the form of what it deems to be uncompensated labor. Specifically, we have in hand the prohibition of factoring in all forms. If a capitalist assigns goods or capital to a storekeeper in exchange for half the profit, the storekeeper in addition must be paid a salary for his attention to that half of the goods, the profit of which accrues to the capitalist. But, Mishnah tractate Baba Mesia 5:5 states, if one hands over cattle to a rancher to raise, in exchange for half the profits, the cattle are deemed to work for their keep, so that rancher need not be paid an additional fee for his labor. One may make an advance agreement on the value of the herd, when the herd yields labor for the benefit of the rancher. Mishnah tractate Baba Mesia 5:6, 5:7, finally, prohibits the arrangement of a farmer's tending a flock on "iron terms," that is to say, on such terms that the owner of the flock is guaranteed a return of all his capital, specified at the outset, and in addition a fixed yield, while the rancher will receive

---

[4]The notion of true value is a separate consideration and another expression of the same notion, namely, the only right exchange is an even one, in which one party does not emerge from the transaction wealthier than before, the other poorer.

the increase of the flock over and above these two fixed items. Thus the rancher, bearing the entire risk for the upkeep of the flock, shares only part of the profits thereof. Israelites may pay or exact interest from gentiles. The notion of risk-capital as risk is rejected. Aristotle will have found himself entirely at home in the premises of these rules.

Once more, the connection between one thing and something else is via Aristotle's theory of wealth and increase. For Mishnah tractate Baba Mesia 5:7-10 goes on to deal with not usury in any sense, but rather agreements on futures and other aspects of increase. One may not agree to pay in advance a fixed sum for a certain amount of produce, if a market price is not yet available. But the market price is administered, not set by the market itself; rather, it is announced and adhered to, as the produce of a given sort reaches the market. No one is supposed to speculate on that matter, and that is the mark of a distributive, not a market, conception of the economy. What follows from speculation? It is that something other than an agreed-upon price is determinative. All of this is translated downward into the (mere) prohibition of usury, but, we realize, here again "usury" simply stands for market economics. If the produce should prove to be more expensive, then the one who receives the money will lose out and turn out to have paid interest on the advance money. Once there is a market price, one may pay in advance for delivery later on; one enjoys an unfair advantage in exchange for his payment in advance. Mishnah tractate Baba Mesia 5:8-9 deals with a loan to be repaid in kind.

Once more barter imposes its conceptions upon the market, which means a *kor* of wheat stands for a *kor* of wheat, without regard to market conditions, which are inadmissible in evidence. In general if one borrows a *kor* of wheat, he cannot pledge to repay a *kor* of wheat. It may turn out that he will have to pay much more for the *kor* than it cost at the time of the loan. This is interest. One may lend his tenant farmers a *kor* of wheat for seed, however, and receive at the end a *kor* of wheat. That is deemed an investment by the landlord in his own property. If one presently owns a *kor* of wheat but has not got access to it, on the other hand, he may agree to return a *kor* later on for one he now receives, without scruple as to violating the laws of interest. That survey suffices to make the simple point that the theory of "usury" and Aristotle's theory of wealth, including usury, exhibit remarkable congruence. Beyond that point we need not go.

A.   What is interest, and what is increase [which is tantamount to taking interest]?
B.   What is interest?
C.   He who lends a *sela* [which is four *denars*] for [a return of] five *denars*,
D.   two *seahs* of wheat for [a return of] three –
E.   because he bites [off too much (NW'SK)].
F.   And what is increase (TRBYT)?
G.   He who increases (HMRBH) [profits] [in commerce] in kind.

H. How so?

I. [If] one purchases from another wheat at a price of a golden *denar* [twenty-five *denars*] for a *kor*, which [was then] the prevailing price, and [then wheat] went up to thirty] *denars*.

J. [If] he said to him, "Give me my wheat, for I want to sell it and buy wine with the proceeds" –

K. [and] he said to him, "Lo, your wheat is reckoned against me for thirty *denars,* and lo, you have [a claim of] wine on me" –

L. but he has no wine.

M.5:1

The formal structure is clear, with its prologue, A, then a systematic commentary on A at B+C-E, F+G-L. The Mishnah clearly has Lev 25:35-6 in mind, since it alludes to the biblical word-choices, N'SK and TRBYT. But the remainder of the chapter is satisfied to refer solely to interest, or usury, as RBYT, which is translated "interest" or "usury" as the case requires. So M.5:1 is essentially secondary to the linguistic and conceptual core of the chapter as a whole, which hardly refers to the distinction announced at the outset. The meaning of interest is clear as given. It involves a repayment of 25 percent over what is lent in cash, or 50 percent over what is lent in kind. Increase is less clear. We deal with a case of trading in futures. The purchaser agrees to pay at the current price of twenty-five *denars* for a *kor;* delivery is postponed until the harvest. Mishnah tractate Baba Mesia 5:7 permits this procedure. When the purchaser calls his contract, the vendor concurs in revising the price of the contract. But he also revises the cost of wine upward to its then-prevailing price. In point of fact, the seller has no wine for sale. This would appear, in contemporary terms, to be trading in 'naked' or uncovered futures. If that is at issue, the prohibition would be based upon the highly speculative character of the vendor's trading practices. But the "increase" is that the vendor now has to pay for the wine at a higher price than is coming to the purchaser.

A. He who lends money to his fellow should not live in his courtyard for free.

B. Nor should he rent [a place] from him for less [than the prevailing rate],

C. for that is [tantamount to] usury.

D. One may effect an increase in the rent-charge [not paid in advance], but not the purchase-price [not paid in advance].

E. How so?

F. [If] one rented his courtyard to him and said to him, "If you pay me now [in advance], lo, it's yours for ten *selas* a year,

G. "but if [you pay me] by the month, it's a *sela* a month" –

H. it is permitted.

I. [But if] he sold his field to him and said to him, "If you pay me the entire sum now, lo, it's yours for a thousand *zuz*.

J. "But if you pay me at the time of the harvest, it's twelve *maneh* [1,200 *zuz*]" –

K.   it is forbidden.

M.5:2

A-C prohibit interest in kind. D is neatly explained at F-H *versus* I-K. The rent falls due month by month, so there is no fee for "waiting" on the payment, while at I-K there is a 20 percent surcharge for postponing payment, tantamount to mortgage interest. Since the rent falls due only month by month, it is not as if the tenant is gaining an undue advantage. The landlord is handing over two *selas* in exchange for the tenant's paying money which has not yet fallen due. But in the latter case, the seller of the field is owed the money as soon as the sale has been effected. By collecting 20 percent extra some time later, he is receiving interest on money which, in fact, already is owing to him. This is not permitted.

A.   [If] one sold him a field, and [the other] paid him part of the price,
B.   and [the vendor] said to him, "Whenever you want, bring me the rest of the money, and [then] take yours [the field]" –
C.   it is forbidden.
D.   [If] one lent him money on the security of his field and said to him, "If you do not pay me by this date three years hence, lo, it is mine" –
E.   lo, it is his.
F.   And thus did Boethus b. Zonin do, on instruction of sages.

M.5:3

At issue here, in the contrast of A-C, D-E, is a subterfuge for the payment of interest. A-C indicate the possibility, for, as we shall see, either the vendor or the purchaser may prove to be the lender at interest, involving usufruct of the field. All depends upon whether the sale is actually consummated through the payment of the whole of the stipulated price. The case of A-C involves partial payment for a field. Transfer of ownership is postponed until full payment is made. The transfer is dated from the time of the sale. What of the usufruct? The vendor, by the terms of B, will enjoy the usufruct of the field in the meantime. If, then, the sale *is* completed, the vendor will retractively have made use of what in fact turns out to belong to the purchaser from the date of sale. That usufruct is a form of interest on the outstanding balance of the debt. But what if we assign the usufruct of the field to the purchaser? Then, if the sale is *not* completed, the purchaser will turn out to have enjoyed the usufruct of a field from the time of the deposit. The deposit will be returned to him. The usufruct thus will appear to be interest on it. So the terms hide a usurious loan, whether of purchaser-lender to owner-borrower or *vice versa*. The second, and contrasting case, simply permits a loan on security, with the proviso that the security or pledge is transferred to the lender only in the event of default at the end. That is not conceived to be interest. The case at D differs from that at B because the status of the field is not left in doubt. It remains the property of the borrower, who is not represented as a purchaser, just as the lender is not a vendor. So there is no unclarity as to the status of the usufruct, which remains fully in the domain of the borrower. That is why the stated precedent, F, is acceptable.

A. They do not set up a storekeeper for half the profit,
B. nor may one give him money to purchase merchandise [for sale] at [the return of the capital plus] half the profit,
C. unless one [in addition] pay him a wage as a worker.
D. They do not set the hens [of another person to hatch one's own eggs] in exchange for half the profit.
E. and they do not assess [and commission another person to rear calves or foals] for half the profit,
F. unless one pay him a salary for his labor and his upkeep.
G. But [without fixed assessment] they accept calves or foals [for rearing] for half the profits,
H. and they raise them until they are a third grown –
I. and as to an ass, until it can carry [a burden] [at which point profits are shared].

M.5:4

The conception before us involves interest in the form of personal service, which also is prohibited. The case has a man commission a tradesman to sell goods in his shop and take half of the profits. But the condition is that, if the goods are lost or destroyed, the tradesman has to bear responsibility for half of the loss. Even if the stock depreciates, the tradesman makes it up at full value. Half of the commission, therefore, is in fact nothing but a loan in kind, for which the tradesman bears full responsibility. It follows that his personal service in selling the owner's half of the stock, if not compensated, in fact is a kind of interest in labor on that loan. D, E, and G, restate this matter in the context of a factor, who commissions a farmer to raise his cattle. At D the man gives eggs to a fowl-keeper, who is to have them hatched. The keeper receives half the profits. He also bears full responsibility for half the loss. It follows that he must be paid a salary. At E, we make an assessment of the value of the calves or foals. Half of this sum becomes the fixed responsibility of the cattle-rancher. If the calves or foals die or depreciate, the rancher has to pay back that sum. So it is a loan in kind. If in addition he is not compensated for time spent taking care of the cattle-factor's share of the herd, once more his work will constitute interest. If, G-H, there is no assessment in advance of the fixed value for which the rancher bears full responsibility, however, then there is a genuine partnership. The rancher receives half the value of the profit. He acknowledges no responsibility for their loss, so there is no loan here. The conditions of the contract are such that the man's labor is amply compensated by his participation in the potential profits on half the herd.

A. They assess [and put out for breeding] a cow, an ass, or anything which works for its keep,

B.   for half the profits.
C.   In a locale in which they are accustomed to divide up the offspring forthwith, they divide it forthwith.
D.   In a place in which they are accustomed to raise the offspring, they raise it.
E.   Rabban Simeon b. Gamaliel says, "They assess [and put out] a calf with its dam, a foal with its dam."
F.   (And) one may pay increased rent [in exchange for a loan for the improvement of] one's field,
G.   and one need not scruple by reason of interest.

M.5:5

The one who supplies the capital, in the form of the cow or ass, benefits from the work of the rancher in raising the animal. But, unlike the case of Mishnah tractate Baba Mesia 5:4D-F, since the animal works for its keep, the rancher gains the usufruct of the animal and so cannot be thought to pay "interest" to the capitalist in exchange for his share in the capital, namely, in the profits on the animals when they are sold. The rancher gets the work of the beast in return both for what he feeds it and his own work with it, so that the considerations of Mishnah tractate Baba Mesia 5:4 are not invoked. C-D provide a minor qualification. Simeon even goes so far, E, as to permit the offspring of a dam to be assessed and raised, even though it is only the dam which will work. F-G, which are separate, complete the list of permissible investments. The point of F-G is that the increased capital investment in the land may yield an increased fee to the landowner for use of the land, without scruple as to usury.

A.   They do not accept from an Israelite a flock on 'iron terms' [that the one who tends the flock shares the proceeds of the flock but restores the full value of the flock as it was when it was handed over to him],
B.   because this is interest.
C.   But they do accept a flock on 'iron terms' from gentiles.
D.   And they borrow from them and lend to them on terms of interest.
E.   And so is the rule for the resident alien.
F.   An Israelite may lend out the capital of a gentile on the say-so of the gentile,
G.   but not on the say-so of an Israelite. [If the gentile had borrowed money from an Israelite, one may not lend it out on interest with the Israelite's knowledge and consent.]

M.5:6

We continue the interest of the foregoing. Terms of "iron flock" are such as to guarantee to the investor both full restitution of capital and a fixed return on the capital. Unlike the conditions at Mishnah tractate Baba Mesia 5:4-5, the rancher undertakes to share in the profit but to bear the full burden of loss. This arrangement involves "interest" in the form of unequal risk. There must be a full participation in both profit and loss in any shared undertaking involving the investment of capital – the animals – on one party's part and of labor and grazing land on the other party's part. (It goes without saying that the perspective of the Mishnah is that of the rancher.) C-D are linked to the foregoing in detail only, but in theme they proceed to conclude the entire discussion of interest. Their point is that the stated prohibition of Mishnah tractate Baba Mesia 5:1-5 applies solely to transactions among Israelites. Gentiles may receive or pay interest. Israelites may work for gentiles in this context. G's language is obscure. It may mean that gentiles may not borrow funds from Israelites and then, through the medium of an Israelite factor, lend them to other Israelites. Or G may wish to say that on his own initiative an Israelite may not lend on interest money belonging to a gentile. The main point is clear.

A. They do not strike a bargain for the price of produce before the market price is announced.
B. [Once] the market price is announced, they strike a bargain,
C. for even though this one does not have [the produce for delivery], another one will have it.
D. [If] one was the first among the reapers [of the given crop], he may strike a bargain with him
E. for (1) grain [already] stacked [on the threshing floor],
F. or for (2) a basket of grapes,
G. or for (3) a vat of olives,
H. or for (4) the clay balls of a potter,
I. or for (5) lime as soon as the limestone has sunk in the kiln.
J. And one strikes a bargain for the price of manure every day of the year.
K. R. Yosé says, "They do not strike a bargain for manure before the manure is on the dung heap."
L. And sages permit.
M. And one may strike a price at the height [of the market, the cheapest rate prevailing at the time of delivery].
N. R. Judah says, "Even though one has not made a bargain at the cheapest rate [prevailing at the time of delivery], one may say to him, 'Give it to me at such-and-such a rate, or give me back my money.'"

M.5:7

What we have here is a denial of the market mechanism as a medium for establishing the price, e.g., in response to demand and supply. Instead we have the theory of distributive economics, in which an authority other than the market dictates prices, hence, the disposition of scarce resources. In the context of usury, there is no point of relevance to the matter at hand. But in the setting of Aristotle's theory of the matter, there is a natural connection. We take up the second general theme of Mishnah tractate Baba Mesia 5:1, "increase." The case before us involves a prepayment for merchandise, e.g., produce. If the merchandise or produce is not yet on the market, one may not strike a price for delivery and accept prepayment on the contract. For this smacks of "increase," in line with M.5:1 – trading in "naked" contracts for futures. When a market price is available, then prepayment may be accepted for later delivery, B-C. As we shall see, Judah, N, maintains that that price must be assumed to be the lowest available, that is to say, either the price at the time of the agreement or the price at the time of the delivery, whichever is lower. The Mishnah will spell this matter out in a principal generalization, A-C, a secondary and gray area, D-I, a special problem, J-L, and then a concluding qualification, M-N, the whole a most interesting exposition. The main objection to trading in futures in the form of "naked calls" is that it smacks of usury. Why? First, The seller of the contract has the use of the money without clear knowledge of what his ultimate costs will be. Second, the buyer of the contract has no protection from the seller's default, should the produce not be available to the seller of the call, all in line with M.5:1. That is why one cannot undertake to deliver a quantity of produce at a given price, unless there is some indication of the prevailing market price for the produce. B-C complete the thought of A. Even though a given farmer has not harvested his crop, he may sell what he is going to harvest, since now there is clear evidence as to what he will receive and what the purchaser should have to pay. In the case of crop failure, the farmer can make it up, C.

D-I present a secondary qualification of foregoing rule. The prohibition of A pertains to crops which both have not been harvested, and also have not been subjected to a prevailing market price. If crops have been harvested, even though there is no prevailing market, one may strike a bargain. Why? Because the crops are now in hand and nearly ready for delivery. There is no possibility of trading in futures as "naked calls." D bears five illustrations. The items are not fully manufactured. So there is an agreement to make delivery later on. The market price may go up. The prepayment, however, is not deemed to fall into the category of interest, in line with Mishnah tractate Baba Mesia 5:1's conception, because it is lower. So what D-I treat is a gray area between crops which are still in the field (Mishnah tractate Baba Mesia 5:1) and those which are fully harvested and ready for delivery (Mishnah tractate Baba Mesia 5:7M-N). There is no market for the former. The market price is set for the latter. There will be a lower price, when prepayment is involved, for partially completed produce, and, as we see, this is all right.

J-K go on to deal with what is always in production. J's view is that the market price is perpetual. Yosé regards the manure as subject to a process of preparation, and L repeats the theory of J. M-N are important. M allows striking a price at the height of the market, when the produce is cheap. The vendor then agrees to supply the produce through the year at the lowest prevailing price for each delivery. This is an important qualification of A, since the market price is now set as a maximum, not a minimum – the theory of D-I all over again. Judah fundamentally concurs and carries the conception still further. Even though we have assumed that we speak of an advance payment at a fixed rate, Judah holds that that fact is always implied, even when it is not stipulated. The purchaser has the right to retract the sale if the lowest prevailing price is not allowed.

A. A man may lend his tenant farmers wheat [to be repaid in] wheat, [if] it is for seed,

B. but no [if it is] for food.

C. For Rabban Gamaliel would lend his tenant farmers wheat [to be repaid in] wheat [when it was used] for seed.

D. [If one lent the wheat when the price was] high and [wheat] became cheap,

E. [or if he lent the wheat when the price was] cheap and [wheat] became expensive,

F. he collects from them at the cheapest price,

G. not because that is what the law requires,

H. but because he wished to impose a strict rule upon himself.

M.5:8

A. A man should not say to his fellow, "Lend me a *kor* of wheat, and I'll pay you back at [a *kor* of wheat] at threshing time."

B. But he says to him, "Lend it to me until my son comes [bringing me wheat],"

C. or, "... until I find the key."

D. Hillel prohibits [even this procedure].

E. And so does Hillel say, "A woman should not lend a loaf of bread to her girlfriend unless she states its value in money.

F. "For the price of wheat may go up, and the two women will turn out to be involved in a transaction of usury."

M.5:9

Once more our concern is to avoid setting a price so long in advance that there is the possibility of usurious profit. If someone lends a *kor* of wheat and is to be repaid a *kor* of wheat six months later, then there is the variable that the *kor* of wheat may now be much less or more expensive than the *kor* of wheat later on. Consequently we have to make provision for what is, and is not, permissible, in line with the basic theory of Mishnah tractate Baba Mesia 5:1, 5:7, 5:8 and 5:9 which go over this ground. Mishnah tractate Baba Mesia 5:8A-B make a fundamental distinction between a *kor* of wheat which is invested in the land owned by the lender, and a *kor* of wheat which is consumed by the borrower. The former may be lent with the proviso that it will be returned, in like kind and quantity, at the harvest. Even though it may increase in value, the lender is deemed not to lend but to invest in his own property (same as Mishnah tractate Baba Mesia 5:3F-G), since, after all, he recovers a share in the profit. But if the loan of the wheat is solely for the benefit of the tenant, then it cannot be repaid in kind, for the stated reason. C-H then provide an illustration of this matter. Gamaliel's procedure, C, is worked out at D-F and glossed at G-H. F means to speak separately to D and to E. If wheat was high when he lent it to his tenants for seed, at the harvest, when it is cheaper, he simply collects the same volume of wheat as he had lent. This then is to their advantage. So it is volume for volume. If wheat was cheap when he lent it for seed, and then, in consequence of a poor harvest, the price went up, he collects in return not the same volume of wheat, but the same value as he had lent, thus collecting less wheat than he had lent but wheat worth the same amount of money as he had handed over. This benign procedure must be in mind, even though F is rather succinct and hardly explicit, for otherwise G-H would be meaningless.

Mishnah tractate Baba Mesia 5:9A-C provide for a mode by which the loan may be effected. In line with Mishnah tractate Baba Mesia 5:8A-B, one cannot promise to give back the same volume of wheat. But if he owns that amount of wheat at this time, but e.g., his son is bringing it, or he does not have the key to the granary, he may effect a loan to be repaid in the exact volume, without reference to the variation in price which may take place in the meantime. Hillel prohibits even this procedure, for the reasons stated at F.

The reader may fairly ask why I claim that the sages of the Mishnah fall into the same framework of economic theory as Aristotle. My answer is to point as systemically indicative, in our context of the character of the economics of the Judaism of the Mishnah, to the treatment of the prohibition of usury, a commonplace for all Judaic systems, deriving as it does from the Scripture shared among them all. What makes the chapter systemically indicative is the simple fact that the framers have chosen to expound this topic as they do – this and not some other, this one here and not elsewhere. Were we to ask for systemically active data, deriving from Scripture, in the Judaism of the Essenes of Qumran, we should look in vain for attention to the matter at hand, even though, self-evidently, the Judaism of the Essenes at Qumran rejected usury, and that by definition. To understand why I point as critical to the economics of the Judaism of the Mishnah to materials commonplace in any other Judaism, I cite Joseph Schumpeter:

> In economics as elsewhere, most statements of fundamental facts acquire importance only by the superstructures they are made to bear and are commonplace in the absence of such superstructures.[5]

In the present context, the fact at hand, the prohibition of usury, scarcely prepares us for the importance accorded to that fact by the framers of the Mishnah, an importance indicated by the exegesis and development of the fact into an encompassing principle of economic transactions of exchange. Whatever the possibilities or potentialities of the scriptural prohibition of interest, the actualities at hand testify to the larger systemic bias and traits of the system-makers before us.

But there is a second consideration, and that is one entirely particular to the case at hand and therefore probative. By "usury" Scripture's authorship meant whatever it meant; that is of no interest to us. We have seen in the chapter at hand that the words translated "usury" really refer to a variety of ordinary market

---

[5]Joseph A. Schumpeter, *History of Economic Analysis*, p. 54.

procedures, and "usury" really means "profit." For in the end what is prohibited is not merely interest on a loan, in cash or in kind, but any transaction which leaves one party materially richer than he was when he entered the transaction, even though the other party is no poorer. Not only so, but even the appearance of "usury" or profit must be avoided, as in the following:

> He who sells a house among the houses in walled cities, lo, this person redeems the house forthwith. And he redeems it at any time in twelve months. Lo, this is a kind of usury which is not usury.

M. Arakhin 9:3A-C

The point is that the one who redeems the house during the year does not deduct from what he repays to the purchaser the rent for the use of the house during the period between the sale and the redemption. It therefore appears that the purchaser has had the use of the house in exchange for the use of his money from the time of the sale to the time of redemption. But this is not usury, since usury applies only to a loan, not to a purchase.[6] Another case in point is the absolute prohibition of factoring. Here there is no consideration that the shopkeeper, selling goods on consignment, or the farmer, raising animals for a share in the profit, is going to be poorer than he was before he undertook the contract. Yet factoring is so organized as to prohibit the capitalist, who supplies the goods on consignment or the capital in the form of the young beasts, to make money on the (mere) labor of the trader or farmer. That is profit on investment, not "usury" in any sense in which the word is used today. And, I state the point with emphasis: *Since the same prohibition is invoked for a variety of modes of the increase of capital, we have to take to heart what really is at stake for our system. And that is Aristotle's conception that profit, including, by the way, usury, is unnatural, but barter, encompassing all manner of goods (theoretically including coins, viewed as commodities), is natural.*

Only within that framework do we grasp the full testimony to the systemic economics that the exegesis of "usury" presents to us. And that conception of "usury," encompassing merely the normal working of the market, is identical with that of Aristotle. The main point is simple. Both Aristotle and the authorship of the Mishnah conceived of the economy as one of self-sufficiency, made up as it was of mostly self-sufficient households joined in essentially self-sufficient villages. In such an economy, as defined by the authorship of the Mishnah, the market had no role to play, except as defining an arena for transactions of equal value and worth among households each possessed of a steady-state worth. Since, in such a (fictive) market, no one emerged richer or poorer than he was when he came to market, but all remained precisely as rich or as poor as they were at the commencement of a transaction, we can hardly call

---

[6]See my *History of the Mishnaic Law of Holy Things* (Leiden: E. J. Brill, 1979). IV. *Arakhin. Temurah*, pp. 77-8.

the Mishnah's market a market at all. For the Mishnah's sages legislated for the market in such a way as to intervene and set aside the market mechanism altogether. They favored one that, in due course, we shall identify as distributive.

The ideal market for the framers of the Mishnah conformed to the larger principle of the system as a whole: equivalence of exchange must govern all transactions. To understand that principle, we turn to Aristotle, as expounded by Polanyi:

> Aristotle's argument on "natural trade" in his *Politics* ... rests on the premise that, like other forms of exchange, trade stems from the requirements of self-sufficiency .... Natural trade is a gainless exchange ....

> The Mishnah is imbued with the Old Testament abhorrence of profit or advantage, derived from any transaction between members of the tribe. Its prescriptions shown an obsession with the moral peril of profiteering, even if involuntarily or inadvertently. Equivalents are here deliberately employed as a safeguard against this danger.[7]

The alternative to market economics is a system of redistribution, or distributive economics, such as is presupposed by the system of barter and gainless exchange (that is, a system in which there can be no risk of loss, any more than there can be a profit, because of extrinsic, nonmarket interventions into the market). In such a system scarce goods are collected and allocated not by the market but by some other authority, e.g., political and religious. This system is described very simply as follows: "Redistribution requires central collection and allocation by a higher authority, but can be seen as satisfying the basic unit's need for services and goods which it cannot produce alone by providing an institutionalized channel for the pooling of resources."[8] In the case of the Judaism of the dual Torah in the statement of the Mishnah, distributive economics is represented by the intervention, into the production and disposition of scarce resources, of God's authority through the priesthood. The rationality of distributive economics rests on the conviction of God as the co-owner, with Israel, therefore with Israelite householders, of the holy land. Hence all farmers or householders are joint tenants, with God, in their fields and produce, and that consideration introduces the justification, within the system, for distributive economics. Aristotle will not have understood the theological rationale, but, after three thousand years of systems of distributive economics, from the Sumerians onward, he presented the final statement of antiquity of the theory of distributive economics, just as the world passed into the system of market economics. Aristotle therefore, in all his anachronism, assuredly will have grasped the distributive, not the market,

---

[7]Karl Polanyi, *The Lifelihood of Man*, p. 69.

[8]Sally C. Humphreys, "History, Economics, and Anthropology: The Work of Karl Polanyi," *History & Theory*, 1969, 8:165-212, p. 205.

economic theory of wealth as it is stated, within its larger system, by the authorship of the Mishnah.

Part Three

WHY THERE IS NO SUCH THING AS

"THE JUDAEO-CHRISTIAN TRADITION"

Chapter Seven

Worlds in Collision:
Judaism and Christianity as Different People Talking about Different Things to Different People

When we have described and analyzed a system, we wish to interpret the system by gaining perspective upon it. And the place to stand is outside. But how to emerge? One way is to compare one system to another. A second is to ask how two distinct systems, drawing upon common sources, e.g., holy books, or facing common or parallel problems, relate to one another. In these next three chapters we turn to the issue of how the families of Christian and Judaic religious systems relate to one another. For in the first three centuries A.D., Christian system-builders had to work out a theory of their relationship not only to ancient Israel in the Hebrew Scriptures, but also to the Israel "after the flesh" who endured in their own time. And from the fourth century onward, Judaic system-builders living in the aftermath of the political triumph of Christianity within the Roman Empire had to take seriously that "Israel after the spirit" that, for three hundred years, they had serenly ignored. The issue of the interrelationship of the two sets of religious systems bears contemporary interest as well, because of the broadly held, and socially beneficial, conception that, after all, there really was, and is, a Judaeo-Christian tradition, which encompasses both "Christianity" and "Judaism," and which forms the foundation of Western civilization. That benign conception has led many to suppose that, in their early centuries, the two sets of religious traditions the two religious worlds intersected, even if in collision. But as we shall now see, in general and in detail, these two worlds never met at all; there was no dialogue between them. They were, and remain, utterly different from one another, and in no material way form, from the viewpoint of the history and comparison of religion, a single religious tradition, the "Judaeo-Christian" one.

The earliest Christians were Jews and saw their religion as normative and authoritative: Judaism. A natural question troubling believing Christians, therefore, is why Judaism as a whole remains a religion that believes *other* things, or, as Christians commonly ask, "Why did the Jews not 'accept Christ'?" or "Why, after the resurrection of Jesus Christ, is there Judaism at all?" Often asked negatively, the question turns on why the Jews do not believe, rather than on what they do believe. Yet it is a constructive question even in the context of description and analysis, not religious polemic. For the question leads us deeper into an understanding not only of the differences between one religion and the other, but also of the traits of the religion under study. In other words, it is a question of comparison – even though the question is not properly framed.

The answer to that question is simple: Judaism and Christianity are completely different religions, not different versions of one religion (that of the "Old Testament," or, "the Written Torah," as Jews call it). The two faiths stand for different people talking about different things to different people. Let me spell this out.

The asking of the question – "Why not?" rather than "Why so?" – reflects the long-term difficulty that the one group has had in making sense of the other. And my explanation of the difference between Christianity and Judaism rests on that simple fact. I maintain, as is clear, that each group talked to its adherents about its points of urgent concern, that is, different people talking about different things to different people. Incomprehension marks relations between Judaism and Christianity in the first century, yet the groups were two sectors of the same people.

Each addressed its own agenda, spoke to its own issues, and employed language distinctive to its adherents. Neither exhibited understanding of what was important to the other. Recognizing that fundamental inner-directedness may enable us to interpret the issues and the language used in framing them. For if each party perceived the other through a thick veil of incomprehension, the heat and abuse that characterized much of their writing about one another testifies to a truth different from that which conventional interpretations have yielded. If the enemy is within, if I see only the mote in the other's eye, it matters little whether there is a beam in my own.

The key is this: the incapacity of either group to make sense of the other. We have ample evidence for characterizing as a family quarrel the relationship between the two great religious traditions of the West. Only brothers can hate so deeply, yet accept and tolerate so impassively, as have Judaic and Christian brethren both hated, yet taken for granted, each other's presence. Christianity wiped out unbelievers, but under ordinary circumstances adhered to the doctrine that the Jews were not to be exterminated. Nevertheless, from the first century onward, the echoes of Matthew's Pharisees as hypocrites and John's Jews as murderers poisoned the Christian conscience. Jews grudgingly recognized that Christianity was not merely another paganism. but in their awareness festered Tarfon's allegation that Christians knew God but denied him, knew the Torah but did violence against its meaning. Today we recognize in these implacably negative projections signs of frustration, anger at someone who should know better than to act as he does, a very deep anger indeed.

The authors of the Gospels chose a broad range of enemies for Jesus, and hence for the church. One group, the Pharisees, assumes importance in our eyes out of proportion to its place in the Gospels, because the kind of Judaism that emerges from the first century draws heavily upon the methods and values imputed to the Pharisees in the later rabbinic literature. So let us narrow our discussion from "Judaism," a word that can stand for just about anything, to that group among first-century Judaisms that in the event contributed substantially to the Judaism that later became normative. And when we speak of Christianity, let us, following the same principle, specify a particular aspect of the rich and various belief of the church represented in the writings of the evangelists. That aspect, the common denominator of the Gospels, finds full expression in the simple claim that Jesus Christ came to save humanity. Hence we shall center on the salvific aspect of the Christianity represented by the Gospels (though not by them alone).

The Judaism defined by the system and method of the Pharisees, whom we met in connection with the destruction of the Second Temple by the Romans in 70 addressed the issue of the sanctification of Israel, while Christianity as defined by the evangelists took up the question of the salvation of Israel. Both were expressions of Israel's religion; one spoke of one thing, the other of something else. In retrospect, although they bear some traits in common, the two groups appear in no way comparable. Why not? The Gospels portray the first Christians as the family and followers of Jesus. So, as a social group, Christianity represented at its outset in a quite physical, familial, and genealogical way "the body of Christ." The Pharisees, by contrast, hardly formed a special group at all. It is easier to say what they were not than what they were. How so? Although the Pharisees appear as a political group by the first century in Josephus's writings about Maccabean politics, the Gospels and the rabbinic traditions concur that what made an Israelite a Pharisee was not exclusively or even mainly politics. The Pharisees were characterized by their adherence to certain cultic rules. They were not a member of a family in any natural or supernatural sense. Their social affiliations in no way proved homologous.

Pharisees, some may object, surely appear as a "they," that is, as a discernible type of Israelite. but if they formed some sort of distinct social group, and if that group took shape in various places around the country, we nevertheless cannot point to much evidence about its character. We have no documentation of any kind concerning the social traits of the Pharisees as a group. What we do have is considerable information on certain practices held to characterize and define people who were called Pharisees. If we eat our meals in one way rather than in some other, however, that common practice does not of itself make us a political party or, for that matter, a church: it makes us people who are willing to eat lunch together.

So, as a hypothesis permitting the argument to unfold, let me say that the Christians carried forward one aspect of Scripture's doctrine of Israel, and the Pharisees another. The Hebrew Scriptures represent Israel as one very large family, descended from a single set of ancestors. The Christians adopted that theory of Israel by linking themselves, first of all, to the family of Jesus and his adopted sons, the disciples, and secondly, through him and them to his ancestry – to David, and on backward to Abraham, Isaac, and Jacob (hence the enormous power of the genealogies of Christ.). The next step – the spiritualization of that familiar tie into the conception of the church as the body of Christ – need not detain us. but Scripture did not restrict itself to the idea of Israel as family; it also defined Israel as a kingdom of priests and a holy people. That is the way taken by the Pharisees. Their Israel found commonality in a shared, holy way of life, required of all Israelites – so Scripture held. The Mosaic Torah defined that way of life in both cultic and moral terms, and the prophets laid great stress on the latter. What made Israel holy – its way of life, its moral character – depended primarily on how people lived, not upon their shared genealogy.

Both Christians and Pharisees belonged to Israel but chose different definitions of the term. The Christians saw Israel as a family; the Pharisees saw it as a way of life. The Christians stressed their genealogy; the Pharisees their ethos and ethics. the Christian family held things in common; the holy people held in common a way of life that sanctified them. At issue in the argument between them are positions that scarcely intersect held by groups whose social self-definitions are incongruent.

Christians were a group comprised of the family of Israel, talking about salvation; Pharisees were a group shaped by the holy way of life of Israel, talking about sanctification. The two neither converse nor argue. For groups unlike one another in what, to begin with, defines and bonds them, groups devoid of a common program of debate, have no argument. They are different people talking about different things to different people. Yet, as is clear, neither group could avoid recognizing the other. What ensued was not a discussion, let alone a debate, but only a confrontation of people with nothing in common pursuing programs of discourse that do not in any way intersect. Not much of an argument.

Why were the two groups fundamentally different? Why did each find the other just that – totally other? Certainly we can identify groups within the larger Israelite society through whom the Christian familists and the Pharisaic commensals could have come to compare one another. Since the Essenes of Qumran laid great stress on observing cultic rules governing meals, Pharisees could have debated with them about which rules must be kept, how to do so, and what larger meaning inhered in them. Since the Essenes also emphasized the coming eschatological war and the messianic salvation of Israel, Christians could have conducted an argument with them about who the Messiah would be and when he would come. Christians and Pharisees, we can see, bear comparison in an essentially morphological dimension with the Essenes of Qumran. But in the terms I have defined, they cannot be so compared with one another.

Let me answer the question of the fundamental difference between the two religious traditions by pointing out what really does make parallel the formulation of the Judaism of each. I mean to make a very simple point. Christianity and Judaism each took over the inherited symbolic structure of Israel's religion. Each in fact did work with the same categories as the other. But, in the hands of each, the available and encompassing classification system found wholly new meaning. The upshot was two religions out of one, each speaking within precisely the same categories, but so radically redefining the substance of these categories that conversation with the other became impossible.

The similarity? Christ embodies God, just as the talmudic sage, or rabbi, in later times would be seen to stand for the torah incarnate.

The difference? Christ brought salvation, and, for the ages to come, the talmudic sage promised salvation.

Salvation, in the nature of things, concerned the whole of humanity; sanctification, equally characteristic of its category, spoke of a single nation, Israel. To save, the messiah saves Israel amid all nations, because salvation categorically entails the eschatological dimension, and so encompasses all of history. No salvation, after all, can last only for a little while, or leave space for time beyond itself. To sanctify, by contrast, the sage sanctifies Israel in particular. Sanctification categorically requires the designation of what is holy against what is not holy. To sanctify is to set apart. No sanctification can encompass everyone or leave no room for someone in particular to be holy. One need not be "holier than thou," but the *holy* requires the contrary category, the *not-holy*. So, once more, how can two religious communities understand one another when one raises the issue of the sanctification of Israel, and the other the salvation of the world? Again, different people talking about different things to different people.

Mutual comprehension becomes still more difficult when the familiar proves strange, when categories we think we understand we turn out not to grasp at all. Using the familiar in strange ways was, I maintain, the most formidable obstacle to resolving the Jewish-Christian argument in the first century. Both Christians and Pharisees radically revised existing categories. To understand this total transvaluation of values, let us examine the principal categories of the inherited Israelite religion and culture. Once their picture is clear, we can readily grasp how, in both Christianity and Judaism, each category undergoes revision, both in definition and in content.

We recall the major trends in Judaism that earlier emerged: priests, scribes, and zealots. To these we now return, remembering, of course, that there were other trends of importance as well. The principal Israelite categories are discernible both in the distinct types of holy men whom we know as priests, scribes, and messiahs, and in the definitive activities of cult, school, and government offices, and (ordinarily) the battlefield. Ancient Israel's heritage yielded the cult with its priests, the Torah with its scribes and teachers, and the prophetic and apocalyptic hope for meaning in history and an eschaton mediated by messiahs and generals. From these derive Temple, school, and (in the apocalyptic expectation) battlefield on earth and in heaven.

To seek a typology of the modes of Israelite piety, we must look for the generative symbol of each mode: an altar for the priestly ideal, a scroll of Scripture for the scribal ideal of wisdom, a coin marked "Israel's freedom: year one" for the messianic modality. In each of these visual symbols we perceive things we cannot touch, hearts and minds we can only hope to evoke. We seek to enter into the imagination of people distant in space and time. We must strive to understand the way in which they framed the world, and encapsulated their world view in some one thing: the sheep for the priestly sacrifice, the memorized aphorism for the disciple, the stout heart for the soldier of light. Priest, sage, soldier – each stands for the whole of Israel. When all would meld into one, there would emerge a fresh and unprecedented Judaism, whether among the heirs of Scribes and Pharisees or among the disciples of Christ.

The symbols under discussion – Temple-altar, sacred scroll, victory wreath for the head of the King-Messiah – largely covered Jewish society. We need not reduce them to their merely social dimensions to recognize that on them was founded the organization of Israelite society and the interpretation of its history. Let us rapidly review the social groups envisaged and addressed by the framers of these symbols:

The priest viewed society as organized along structural lines emanating from the Temple. His caste stood at the top of a social scale in which all things were properly organized, each with its correct name and proper place. The inherent sanctity of the people of Israel, through the priests' genealogy, came to its richest embodiment in the high priest. Food set apart for the priests' rations, at God's command, possessed the same sanctity; so, too, did the table at which priests ate. To the priest, for the sacred society of Israel, history was an account of what happened in, and (alas) on occasions to, the Temple.

To the sage, the life of society demanded wise regulations. Relationships among people required guidance by the laws enshrined in the Torah and best interpreted by Scribes; the task of Israel was to construct a way of life in accordance with the revealed rules of the Torah. The sage, master of the rules, stood at the head.

Prophecy insisted that the fate of the nation depended upon the faith and moral condition of society, a fact to which Israel's internal and external history testified. Both sage and priest saw Israel from the viewpoint of externity, but the nation had to live out its life in this world, among other peoples coveting the very same land, and within the context of Roman imperial policies and politics. The messiah's kingship would resolve the issue of Israel's subordinate relationship to other nations and empires, establishing once and for all the desirable, correct context for priest and sage alike.

Implicit in the messianic framework was a perspective on the world beyond Israel for which priest and sage cared not at all. The priest perceived the Temple as the center of the world: beyond it he saw in widening circles the less holy, then the unholy, and further still, the unclean. All lands outside the Land of Israel were unclean with corpse uncleanness; all other peoples were unclean just as corpses were unclean. Accordingly, in the world life abided within Israel; and in Israel, within the Temple. Outside, in the far distance, were vacant lands and dead peoples, comprising an undifferentiated wilderness of death – a world of uncleanness. From such a perspective, no teaching about Israel among the nations, no interest in the history of Israel and its meaning, was apt to emerge.

The wisdom of the sage pertained in general to the streets, marketplaces and domestic establishments (the household units) of Israel. What the sage said was wisdom as much for gentiles as for Israel. The universal wisdom proved international, moving easily across the boundaries of culture and language, from eastern to southern to western Asia. It focused, by definition, upon human experience common to all and undifferentiated by nation, essentially unaffected by the large movements of history. Wisdom spoke about fathers and sons, masters and disciples, families and villages, not about nations, armies, and destiny.

Because of their very diversity these three principal modes of Israelite existence might easily cohere. Each focused on a particular aspect of the national life, and none essentially contradicted any other. One could worship at the Temple, study the Torah, and fight in the army of the Messiah – and some did all three. Yet we must see these modes of being – and their consequent forms of piety – as separate. Each contained its own potentiality to achieve full realization without reference to the others.

The symbolic system of Cult, Torah and messiah demanded choices. If one thing was most important, others must have been less important. Either history matters, or it happens, without significance, "out there." Either the proper conduct of the cult determines the course of the seasons and the prosperity of the Land, or it is "merely ritual" – an unimportant external and not the critical heart. (We hear this judgment in, for example, the prophetic polemic against the cult.) Either the messiah will save Israel, or he will ruin everything. Accordingly, though we take for granted that people could have lived within the multiple visions of priest, sage, and messiah, we must also recognize that such a life was vertiginous. Narratives of the war of 66-73 emphasize that priests warned messianists not to endanger their Temple. Later sages – talmudic rabbis – paid slight regard to the messianic struggle led by Bar Kokhba, and after 70 claimed the right to tell priests what to do.

The way in which symbols were arranged and rearranged was crucial. Symbol change is social change. A mere amalgam of all three symbols hardly serves by itself as a mirror for the mind of Israel. The particular way the three were bonded in a given system reflects an underlying human and social reality. That is how it should be, since, as we saw, the three symbols with their associated myths, the world views they projected, and the way of life they defined, stood for different views of what really matters. In investigating the existential foundations of the several symbolic systems available to Jews in antiquity, we penetrate to the bedrock of Israel's reality, to the basis of the life of the nation and of each Israelite, to the ground of being – even to the existential core that we the living share with them.

Let us unpack the two foci of existence: public history, and the private establishment of the home and heart. We may call the first "time." Its interest is in one-time, unique *events* that happen day by day in the here and now of continuing history. The other focus we may call "eternity." Its interest is in the recurrent and continuing *patterns* of life – birth and death, planting and harvest, the regular movement of the sun, moon, stars in heaven, night and day, Sabbaths, festivals, and regular seasons on earth. The two share one existential issue: How do we respond to the ups and downs of life?

The events of individual life – birth, maturing, marriage, death – do not make history, except for individuals. But the events of group life – the formation of groups, the development of social norms and patterns, depression and prosperity, war and peace – these do make history. When a small people coalesces and begins its course through history in the face of adversity, one of two things can happen. Either the group may disintegrate in the face of disaster and lose its hold on its individual members; or the group may fuse, being strengthened by trial, and so turn adversity into renewal.

The modes around which Israelite human and national existence coalesced – those of priests, sages and messianists (including prophets and apocalyptists) – emerge, we must remember, from national and social consciousness. The heritage of the Written Torah (the Hebrew Scriptures or "Old Testament") was carried forward in all three approaches to Judaism. The Jewish people knew the mystery of how to endure through history. In ancient Israel adversity elicited self-conscious response. Things did not merely *happen* to Israelites. God made them happen to teach lessons to Israel. The prophetic and apocalyptic thinkers in Israel shaped, reformulated, and interpreted events, treating them as raw material for renewing the life of the group.

History was not merely "one damn thing after another." It was important, teaching significant lessons. It had a purpose and was moving somewhere. The writers of Leviticus and Deuteronomy, of the historical books from Joshua through Kings, and of the prophetic literature, agreed that, when Israel did God's will, it enjoyed peace, security, and prosperity; when it did not, it was punished at the hands of mighty kingdoms raised up as instruments of God's wrath. This conception of the meaning of Israel's life produced another question: How long? When would the great events of time come to their climax and conclusion? And as one answer to that question, there arose the hope for the messiah, the anointed of God, who would redeem the people and set them on the right path forever, thus ending the vicissitudes of history.

When we reach the first century A.D., we come to a turning point in the messianic hope. No one who knows the Gospels will be surprised to learn of the intense, vivid, prevailing expectation among some groups that the Messiah was coming soon. Their anticipation is hardly astonishing. People who fix their attention on contemporary events of world-shaking dimensions naturally look to a better future. That expectation is one context for the messianic myth.

More surprising is the development among the people of Israel of a second, quite different response to history. It is the response of those prepared once and for all to transcend historical events and to take their leave of wars and rumors of wars, of politics and public life. These persons, after 70, undertook to construct a new reality beyond history, one that focused on the meaning of humdrum everyday life. We witness among the sages ultimately represented in the Mishnah, neither craven nor exhausted passivity in the face of world-shaking events but the beginnings of an active construction of a new mode of being. They chose to exercise freedom uncontrolled by history, to reconstruct the meaning and ultimate significance of events, to seek a world within ordinary history, a different and better world. They undertook a quest for eternity in the here and now; they strove to form a society capable of abiding amid change and stress. Indeed, it was a fresh reading of the meaning of history. the nations of the world suppose that they make "history" and think that their actions matter. But these sages knew that it is God who makes history, and that it is the reality formed in response to God's will that counts as history: God is the King of kings of kings.

This conception of time and change had, in fact, formed the focus of the earlier priestly tradition, which was continued later in the Judaism called rabbinic or talmudic. This Judaism offered an essentially metahistorical approach to life. It lived above history and its problems. It expressed an intense inwardness. The Judaism attested in the rabbis' canon of writings emphasized the ultimate meaning contained within small and humble affairs. Rabbinic Judaism came in time to set itself up as the alternative to all forms of messianic Judaism – whether in the form of Christianity or militaristic zealotry and nationalism – which claimed to know the secret of history, the time of salvation and the way to redemption. But paradoxically the canonical writings of rabbis also disclosed answers to these questions. The messiah-myth was absorbed into the rabbis' system and made to strengthen it. The rabbinical canon defined in a new way the uses and purposes of all else that had gone before.

This approach to the life of Israel, stressing continuity and pattern and promising change only at the very end, when all would be in order, represents the union of two trends. The one was symbolized by the altar, the other by the Torah scroll, the priest and the sage. In actual fact, the union was effected by a kind of priest manque, and by a special kind of sage. The former was the Pharisee, the latter the scribe.

The scribes were a profession. They knew and taught Torah. They took their interpretation of Torah very seriously, and for them the act of study had special importance. The Pharisees were a sect and had developed a peculiar perception of how to live and interpret life: they acted in their homes as if they were priests in the Temple. Theirs was an "as if" way. They lived "as if" they were priests, "as if" they had to obey at home the laws that applied to the Temple. When the Temple was destroyed in 70, the Pharisees were prepared. They continued to live "as if" there were a new Temple composed of the Jewish people.

These, then represent the different ways in which the great events were experienced and understood. One was the historical-messianic way, stressing the intrinsic importance of events and concentrating upon their weight and meaning. The other was the metahistorical, scribal-priestly-rabbinic way, which emphasized Israel's power of transcendence and the construction of an eternal, changeless mode of being in this world, capable of riding out the waves of history.

We may now return to our starting point, where Judaic and Christian religious life led in different directions. Judaic consciousness in the period under discussion had two competing but not yet "contradictory" symbol systems: the altar/scroll of the Pharisees and scribes; the wreath of the King-Messiah. What made one focus more compelling than the other? The answer emerges when we realize that each kind of piety addressed a distinctive concern; each spoke about different things to different people. We may sort out the types of piety by returning to our earlier observations. Priests and sages turned inward, toward the concrete everyday life of the community. They addressed the sanctification of Israel. Messianists and their prophetic and apocalyptic teachers turned outward, toward the affairs of states and nations. They spoke of the salvation of Israel. Priests saw the world of life in Israel, and death beyond. They knew what happened to Israel without concerning themselves with a theory about the place of Israel among the nations. For priests, the nations formed an undifferentiated realm of death. Sages, all the more, spoke of home and hearth, fathers and sons, husbands and wives, the village and enduring patterns of life. What place was there in this domestic scheme for the realities of history – wars and threats of wars, the rise and fall of empires? The sages expressed the consciousness of a singular society amidst other societies. At issue for the priest/sage was being; for the prophet/messianist the issue was becoming.

The radical claims of the holiness sects, such as Pharisees and Essenes, of professions such as the scribes, and of followers of messiahs – all expressed aspects of Israel's common piety. Priest, scribe, messiah – all stood together with the Jewish people along the same continuum of faith and culture. Each expressed in a particular and intense way one mode of the piety that the people as a whole understood and shared. That is why we can move from the particular to the general in our description of the common faith in first-century Israel. That common faith, we hardly need argue, distinguished Israel from all other peoples of the age, whatever the measure of "Hellenization" in the country's life; as far as Israel was concerned, there was no "common theology of the ancient Near East."

No wonder that the two new modes of defining Judaic piety that issued from the period before 70 A.D. and thrived long after that date – the Judaism framed by sages from before the first to the seventh century, and Christianity with its paradoxical king-messiah – redefined that piety, while remaining true to emphases of the inherited categories. Each took over the established classifications – priest, scribe, and messiah – but infused them with new meaning. Though in categories nothing changed, in substance nothing remained what it had been. That is why both Christian and Judaic thinkers reread the received Scriptures – "the Old Testament" to the one, "the Written Torah" to the other – and produced, respectively, "the New Testament" and the "Oral Torah." The common piety of the people Israel in its land defined the program of religious life for both the Judaism and the Christianity that emerged after the caesura of the destruction of the Temple. The bridge to Sinai – worship, revelation, national and social eschatology – was open in both directions.

Thus Christ as perfect sacrifice, teacher, prophet, and King-Messiah, in the mind of the Church brought together but radically recast the three foci of what had been the common piety of Israel in Temple times. Still later on, the figure of the talmudic sage would encompass but redefine all three categories as well.

How so? After 70, study of Torah and obedience to it became a temporary substitute for the Temple and its sacrifice. The government of the sages in accord with "the one whole Torah of Moses, our rabbi," revealed by God at Sinai, carried forward the scribes' conception of Israel's proper government. The Messiah would come when all Israel, through mastery of the Torah and obedience to it, had formed that holy community which, to begin with, the Torah prescribed in the model of Heaven revealed to Moses at Sinai. Jesus as perfect priest, rabbi, Messiah, was a protean figure. So was the talmudic rabbi as Torah incarnate, priest for the present age, and, in the model of (Rabbi) David, progenitor and paradigm of the messiah. In both cases we find an unprecedented rereading of established symbols.

The history of the piety of Judaism is the story of successive rearrangements and revisioning of symbols. From ancient Israelite times onward, there would be no system of classification beyond the three established taxa. But no category would long be left intact in its content. When Jesus asked people who they thought he was, the enigmatic answer proved less interesting than the question posed. For the task he set himself was to reframe everything people knew through encounter with what they did not know: a taxonomic enterprise. When the rabbis of late antiquity rewrote in their own image and likeness the entire Scripture and history of Israel, dropping whole eras as though they had never been, ignoring vast bodies of old Jewish writing, inventing whole new books for the canon of Judaism, they did the same thing. They reworked what they had received in light of what they proposed to give. No mode of piety could be left untouched, for all proved promising. In Judaism from the first century to the seventh, every mode of piety would be refashioned in the light of the vast public events represented by the religious revolutionaries – rabbi-clerk, rabbi-priest, rabbi-messiah.

Accordingly, the piety of Israel in the first century ultimately defined the structure of the two great religions of Western civilization: Christianity, through its Messiah, for the gentile; Judaism through its definition in the two Torahs of Sinai and in its embodiment in the figure of the sage, for Israel. Once they understand that simple fact, Christians can try to understand Judaism in its own terms – and Jews can do the same for Christianity. For they have, in fact, nothing in common, at least, nothing in common that matters very much.

Chapter Eight

The Absoluteness of Christianity and the Uniqueness of Judaism: Why Salvation Is Not of the Jews

The publication more than a half-century ago of Billerbeck's convenient compendium of ready references in the rabbinic literature to New Testament topics only accelerated the trend, well under way from the end of the nineteenth century, to appeal to rabbinic writings for solutions of intractable problems in New Testament exegesis. These concerned particularly arcane concerns in the writings of Paul and in the Gospels, for instance, the law in Paul, the doctrine of the Messiah and salvation in the Gospels. Indeed, it was said that if a saying could be shown to be "Jewish" and not "Greek," then Jesus really said it. Stated with more probity, the position was simple. People expected to find in the writings of Judaism pretty much the way things were, and that would permit them to make sense of what Paul and the Evangelists had to say. They wished to read the letters and stories as arguments with opponents accurately represented as to their opinions, outsiders who stood for other positions, framed in their own terms, subject to criticism and rejection by the nascent faith. Christianity then came to be represented as a kind of reform of Judaism, not as an absolute and autonomous religion on its own.

Not only so, but the incipient movement in the rapprochement of Judaism and Christianity in the twentieth century, made urgent by the catastrophe, to the Jews, of World War II, added impetus to the movement. Consequently, debates on the covenantal nature of "the law," or on the conception of law in "Judaism," flourish not in rabbinical but in Christian theological circles. The contemporary impasse in Pauline studies draws attention to arcane matters of concern not to Paul and those who preserved and canonized his writings, but to those whose reading of the Old Testament covenant Paul tells us that he rejected. By now it has become increasingly evident that to understand Paul's view of "Judaism," we have to understand (only) Paul, there being no Judaism "out there," attested by sources outside of the Pauline corpus, that appeals to classifications and categories common to those of Paul and so available for comparison with Paul's picture. And that leads us to a theological judgment with implications for the interpretation of both Christian and Judaic writings of late antiquity.

It is the simple point that Christianity is absolute, and Judaism is unique (to use the correct language of their respective theologies). In fact there can be no dialogue between an entity that is *sui generis* and any other entity, and, given the correct insistence of Christianity on its absoluteness and of Judaism on its uniqueness, genuine dialogue falls beyond the limits of logical discourse. The implications for New Testament hermeneutics will prove self-evident. The blurring of the boundaries between the one and the other, the representation of Christianity as a kind of Judaism, the appeal to Judaism for validation and judgment of (a) Christianity – these familiar traits of contemporary biblical and theological studies obscure that simple fact. Christianity began on the first Easter. It is, therefore, absolute in its reading of its circumstance and context.

Christianity is not a kind of Judaism, and it is not a continuation of "the Judaeo-Christian tradition," any more than Judaism in any statement forms a prior or correlative religious tradition with or in relationship to Christianity. In comparison to the other, each one is wholly other. The absolute standing of Christianity finds expression in its view that the words incarnation and gospel can be spelled only with a capital I and a capital G, respectively. In all time and in eternity, there have been, and can be, only one, unique, absolute Incarnation, that of Jesus Christ, raised from the dead, and only one Gospel, the Gospel of the salvation of Jesus Christ. To the Gospels Judaism in all forms is simply not much to the point.

The Judaic writings that have become normative as the Judaism of the dual Torah lay claim, by no means alone among Judaisms, to the counterpart position, namely, the uniqueness of "Israel," meaning, the Jewish People after the flesh. Like the G and the I, the "p" is capitalized, because there is only that one People in the genus which it defines; all other peoples are a different genus of people altogether. The experience of Jewry forms a history that is continuous, however disjointed, and that also takes place out of phase with all other peoples' histories. Genesis Rabbah, one of the monuments of rabbinic biblical exegesis, represents "Israel" as the counterpart to Adam, and Israel's history as the counterpart to the story of Eden. Adam's fall led to the ultimate degradation of humanity, and the restoration began with Abraham and reached its conclusion at Sinai with Moses and Israel. To Christian theologians the picture is a familiar one, with Jesus Christ as the last Adam, serving, as "Israel" does in the theology of Judaism, as the centerpiece of the claim of absolute-ness (Christian) or unique-ness (Judaic). And, we know in the history and comparison of religion, that component of a religious system that a religion identifies as unique, therefore beyond all sharing or communication with outsiders, brings us to the center of matters.

In that context, the premise that the holy books of Christianity are to be read in light of Judaic counterparts forms an odd and jarring conviction. When, to revert to the example of Paul, people appeal to Judaic writings, of any setting and of any period of composition, even long after the first century, to explain what Paul can have meant by the law, they violate not only rules of historical relevance. They disrupt, also, the natural flow of theological thinking. The reason is that they assume a continuity where there has been, and can only have been, a radical break; they bridge an abyss beyond all reckoning. The upshot is to assume that people can have understood one another, who, in point of fact, have no language in common.

Before giving instances of that fact, let me hasten to introduce an important distinction in the analysis of the relationships between religious systems. It is between a fact that is systemically vital, and one that is inert. For the study of economics, this point has been made by Joseph A. Schumpeter as follows: "In economics as elsewhere, most statements of fundamental facts acquire importance only by the superstructures they are made to bear and are commonplace in the absence of such superstructures."[1]

That is to say, a system of religious thought, comprising a world view, a way of life, and a definition of the social entity meant to adopt the one and embody the other, makes ample use of available facts. In order to make their statement, the authors of the documents of such a system speak in a language common to their age. Some of these facts form part of the background of discourse, like the laws of gravity. They are, if important, inert, because they bear no portion of the burden of the systemic message. I call such facts inert. Other of these facts form centerpieces of the system; they may or may not derive from the common background. Their importance to the system forms part of the statement and testimony of that system. The fact that the legal requirements of the Jews of Palestine ("Israel" in the "land of Israel") of the first century insisted upon a writ of divorce when a marriage came to an end is critical in understanding debates on correct grounds for divorce. But it is an inert, not a systemically active, fact. We have to know that fact, but, when we do, we still have not properly entered into the systemic importance (if any) of sayings on acceptable grounds for divorce.

Let me give one unimportant example of the difference between an inert and a systemically vital fact, drawn from my own research,[2] though whole encyclopaedias of New Testament exegesis exemplify the same fact. To understand the saying, "First cleanse the inside" (Lk. 11:39, Mt. 23:25-6), we have to know that in someone's purity rules of the time in which the saying took shape, people treated as different domains, as to cultic uncleanness, the inside of a goblet and the outside of the same goblet. Without knowing that fact, the saying is gibberish. But knowing that fact does not help us to understand what Jesus (really) said or even meant. That fact is inert, forming the background for the statement that the saying wishes to make. But the sense of

---

[1]Joseph A. Schumpeter, *History of Economic Analysis*, p. 54.
[2]*A History of the Mishnaic Law of Purities* (Leiden: E. J. Brill, 1974) III. Kelim, pp. 374ff.

the statement and its message derive from the theological context of the evangelists, which, for Luke, addresses a different issue ("Give for alms those things which are within"), from that critical to Matthew, whose gospel aims at underlining the critique of scribes and Pharisees as hypocrites ("First cleanse the inside ... that the outside also may be clean"). The inert fact contains valuable information for the study of a Judaism of the period of the Gospels, as a matter of fact, for, as I have shown elsewhere, the Gospels' sayings presuppose a legal situation that differs from the rule that forms the premise for the rabbinic text in which the rule appears. The upshot is that we cannot understand the "First cleanse the inside" sayings without knowing "Judaism." But when we do know "Judaism," we still do not understand those sayings. For the use of the fact of "Judaism" testifies to the systemic intent and makes the system's statement, and that statement has no bearing whatever on the fact that is used. That is, then, an inert fact: interesting, but not very consequential. The case at hand therefore forms ample evidence for the importance, for understanding Judaism, of the Christian "background" ("Umwelt"), as much as, it is commonly maintained, understanding Christianity requires knowledge of the Jewish or Judaic "background." But, in the nature of things, the same evidence testifies to the unimportance of knowing about Judaism for interpreting the Gospels, and of knowing about Christianity for interpreting the law.

For neither is effectively the background for the other. When we come to systemically critical facts, there is not only no continuity let alone confrontation, but not even a connection. The criterion for connection surely derives from comprehension. For continuities to be established, such that, interpreting a systemic detail in one system permits us to make sense of a systemic detail of another system entirely, we require some kind of dialogue, at least a confrontation. But what if we notice that one group simply cannot make sense of the message of the other? Then we have to call into question our premise that the system of the one presupposes not only facts, but the systemic statement, fully comprehended, of the other. People maintain that we cannot understand Christianity (in any form) if we do not understand Judaism (in all forms, e.g., Essene and Philonic and Rabbinic and what have you). They take as an article of academic conviction that Christianity was born out of Judaism, and they present as a foundation of contemporary interreligious dialogue that Christianity forms the daughter-religion of Judaism.[3] But I shall now show, first through a case, then through general observations, that Judaism (in the

---

[3]But the ecumenical movement that encompasses Christianity and Islam and Christianity and Buddhism does not insist upon the same intersections, e.g., that Christianity can be understood only in the context of Muhammed's life and teachings or Buddha's. So there can be such interreligious dialogue as is possible without those foundations that scholarship, distinct from theology, is supposed to be able to lay down. But I do not see a future for religious dialogue between Christianity and Judaism until each party understands that it cannot understand what is unique to the other, which is to say, what makes the other other.

system that became normative) and Christianity (in Gospels that became canonical) represent different people talking about different things to different people, with no possibility of mutual comprehension, let alone dialogue.

My particular case of the impossibility of mutual comprehension derives from Mk. 11:15-19, the driving of the money-changers out of the temple. With commendable confidence, some exegetes maintain that the sense and meaning of Jesus's action will have been immediately comprehensible and self-evident. Jesus will have been understood to have attacked the Temple. I shall try to show the opposite: Jesus will not have been understood at all, hence will have been regarded as a mere madman. It is correctly alleged[4] that the money-changers performed an essential service: "The money-changers were probably those who changed the money in the possession of pilgrims into the coinage acceptable by the temple in payment of the half-shekel tax levied on all Jews."[5] They charged a fee for doing so. In order to purchase animals for sacrifice, pilgrims had to pay the appropriate fee, and the money-change made it possible, again Sanders: "The business arrangements around the temple were necessary if the commandments were to be obeyed." Interpreting this action of Jesus, Sanders says that it symbolized destruction: "That is one of the most obvious meanings of the action of overturning itself."[6] Sanders states his interpretation in this way:

> Thus we conclude that Jesus publicly predicted or threatened the destruction of the temple, that the statement was shaped by his expectation of the arrival of the eschaton, that he probably also expected a new temple to be given by God from heaven, and that he made a demonstration which prophetically symbolized the coming event.[7]

Sanders's interpretation is not at issue. What I wonder is whether, to Jews familiar with Scripture and the understanding of Scripture embodied in the Temple, the action will have had any obvious meaning at all. To find out, we turn to a later document, for reasons that will become clear presently. If we ask the authorship of the Mishnah, ca. A.D. 200, to tell us why the money-changers were in the Temple, they would give us a simple answer:

A. On the fifteenth of that same month [Adar, before Nisan] they set up money-changers' tables in the provinces.
B. On the twenty-fifth of Adar they set them up in the Temple.
C. Once they were set up in the Temple, they began to exact pledges from those who had not paid the tax in specie.
D. From whom do they exact a pledge?

---

[4]See the excellent discussion by E. P. Sanders on "Jesus and the Temple" in his *Jesus and Judaism* (Philadelphia: Fortress Press, 1985), pp. 61-76.
[5]Sanders, p. 64.
[6]Sanders, p. 70.
[7]Sanders, p. 75.

E.   Levites, Israelites, proselytes, and freed slaves, but not from women, slaves, and minors.

M. Sheqalim 1:3

Money-changers serve to change diverse coinage into the sheqel required for the Temple tax. They would take a place from one who has not yet paid his tax and in exchange supply the required half-sheqel. They were essentially for the collection of the tax. Why? I state with emphasis: *Because that tax, paid by all eligible Israelites, serves through the coming year to provide the public daily whole-offerings in the name of the community.* Those who did not have to pay the tax could do so, e.g., women, slaves, or minors. But a gentile or a Samaritan could not pay the tax. They could contribute freewill offerings, but they could not participate in supplying the Temple tax of a half-sheqel. Thus far I go over the familiar consensus, as accurately portrayed by Sanders.

What is at stake in the changing of money is a very considerable consideration, which pertains only to Israelite males as obligatory, other Israelites as voluntary. And what was that? To understand the place of the money-changers in the Temple we require an answer to that question. It is supplied by the authorship of the Tosefta, an amplification of the Mishnah brought to closure about ca. A.D. 300, a century after the closure of the Mishnah.[8]

A.   *Once they were set up in the Temple, they began to exact pledges from those who had not yet paid [M. Sheqalim 1:3C].*
B.   They exact pledges from Israelites for their sheqels, so that the public offerings might be made [paid for] by using their funds.
C.   This is like a man who got a sore on his foot, and the doctor had to force it and cut off his flesh so as to heal him. Thus did the Holy One, blessed be he, exact a pledge from Israelites for the payment of their sheqels, so that the public offerings might be made out of their funds.
D.   For public offerings appease and effect atonement between Israel and their father in heaven.
E.   Likewise we find of the heave-offering of sheqels which the Israelites paid in the wilderness, as it is said, "And you shall take the atonement money from the people of Israel and shall appoint it for the service of the tent of meeting, that it may bring the people of Israel to remembrance before the Lord, so as to make atonement for yourselves" (Ex. 30:16).

Tosefta Sheqalim 1:6[9]

---

[8]This seems to me not yet fully appreciated in the available literature, ably summarized by Sanders.
[9]I have presented the entire textual representation in my *History of the Mishnaic Law of Appointed Times* (Leiden: E. J. Brill, 1982). III. *Sheqalim, Yoma, Sukkah. Translation and Explanation*, pp. 8-15.

The proof text, Ex. 30:16, explicitly links the sheqel-offering in the wilderness to the sheqel-tax or offering in the Temple. Both attained atonement for sin. Not only so, but the parable, C, makes the matter explicit. The doctor has to cut off the flesh so as to heal the patient. The sin is the sore on the foot. The doctor has to force the sore and cut it off. The Holy One has to exact the pledge of the half-sheqel so as to make all Israelites responsible for the daily whole-offerings, which atone for Israel's sin. The explanation for the payment of the sheqel-tax forms a chapter in the larger conception of the daily whole-offerings, a chapter commenced by Ex. 30:16's explicit statement that the daily whole-offering atones for the sin of each Israelite and all Israel every day. These daily whole-offerings, it is clear, derive from communal funds, provided by every Israelite equally. They serve all Israelites individually and collectively, as atonement for sin.

And to the accomplishment of that holy purpose, the money-changers, as a matter of fact, were simply essential. They formed an integral part in the system of atonement and expiation for sin.[10] The explicit explanation of the payment of the half-sheqel, therefore, is that it allowed all Israelites to participate in the provision of the daily whole-offering, which accomplished atonement for sin in behalf of the holy people as a whole. That explains why gentiles and Samaritans may not pay the sheqel, while women, slaves, or minor Israelites may do so (M. Sheqalim 1:5A-B). For gentiles and Samaritans do not form part of "Israel," and therefore are unaffected by the expiation accomplished by the daily whole-offering.

Now to the point at hand. Some maintain that everyone will have understood the meaning of Jesus's action. But I think the contrary is the fact. Anyone who understood that conception of the daily whole-offering will have found incomprehensible and unintelligible an action of overturning the tables of the money-changers. Such an action will have provoked astonishment, since it will have called into question the very simple fact that the daily whole-offering effected atonement and brought about expiation for sin, and God had so instructed Moses in the Torah. Accordingly, only someone who rejected the Torah's explicit teaching concerning the daily whole-offering could have overturned the tables – or, as I shall suggest, someone who had in mind setting up a different table, and for a different purpose: for the action carries the entire message, both

---

[10]Can we impute wide circulation in the first century to the contents of a statement of the Tosefta in amplification of the Mishnah, an authorship of ca. A.D. 300 addressing a document of ca. A.D. 300? In this instance, there is a simple reason for thinking so. Since Ex. 30:16 is explicit in the matter, I am not inclined to doubt that the interpretation of the atoning power and expiatory effect of the daily whole-offering circulated in the first century. On the contrary, if Scripture is explicit, then people will have known the meaning of the rite; it was a commonplace. And, for the same reason, I see no grounds for doubting that people generally grasped the reason for the presence of the money-changers, who, as is clear, simply facilitated an essential rite of all Israel.

negative and positive. Indeed, the money changers' presence made possible the cultic participation of every Israelite, and it was not only not a blemish on the cult but part of its perfection. That is why I doubt that anyone can have understood what Jesus did, except, of course, Jesus and his disciples. The gesture was in context simply beyond all comprehension.

We have to work our way back from the purpose of the daily whole-offering to the task of the money-changers in order to understand the statement made by Jesus through his action. And, it must follow, as I said, that no Jew of the time who deemed the Temple the place where Israel atoned for sin can have understood the meaning of the action of Jesus, because nearly all Jews both in the land of Israel and in the Exile took for granted that the daily whole-offerings expiated sin and so restored the relationship between God and Israel that sin spoiled. But I have also to add that everyone who grasped the context of Jesus's action will have appreciated the statement made by his action. That context was the establishment of the Eucharist, the rite of atonement and expiation of sin that Jesus would found within that same Passion narrative to which the action before us formed a prologue – but also a counterpart.

For the overturning of the money-changers' tables represents an act of the rejection of the most important rite of the Israelite cult, the daily whole-offering, and, therefore, a statement that there is a means of atonement other than the daily whole-offering, which now is null. Then what was to take the place of the daily whole-offering? It was to be the rite of the Eucharist: table for table, whole-offering for whole-offering. It therefore seems to me that the correct context in which to read the overturning of the money-changers' tables is not the destruction of the Temple in general, but the institution of the sacrifice of the Eucharist, in particular. It further follows that the counterpart of Jesus's negative action in overturning one table must be his affirmative action in establishing or setting up another table, that is to say, I turn to the Passion narratives centered upon the Last Supper. That, at any rate, is how, as an outsider to scholarship in this field, I should suggest we read the statement. The negative is that the atonement for sin achieved by the daily whole-offering is null, and the positive, that atonement for sin is achieved by the Eucharist: one table overturned, another table set up in place, and both for the same purpose of atonement and expiation of sin. When we realize how the central actions in Jesus's life, as contemporary scholarship identifies them, first, the driving out of the money-changers, second, the institution of the Eucharist, correspond with one another, and when we recall how broadly the understanding of the daily whole-offering will have circulated among Jews in general, we realize the utter incomprehensibility of Christianity, in its initial stages and statement, in the context of Judaism. The two religious traditions, Christianity and Judaism, in their first statements, really do represent different people talking about different things to different people.

This simple case may now lead to a broader generalization. I maintain, as is clear, that each group talked to its adherents about its points of urgent concern, that is, different people talking about different things to different people.[11] Incomprehension marks relations between Judaism and Christianity in the first century, even though the groups were two sectors of the same people. The reason is that each addressed its own agenda, spoke to its own issues, and employed language distinctive to its adherents. Neither exhibited understanding of what was important to the other.

The authors of the Gospels chose a broad range of enemies for Jesus, and hence for the Church. And, we recognize, there also was no Orthodox or single Judaism. To show the improbability of mutual comprehension, let me focus upon one group, the Pharisees. That group assumes importance in our eyes out of proportion to its place in the Gospels, because the kind of Judaism that emerges from the first century draws heavily upon the methods and values imputed to the Pharisees in the later rabbinic literature. When we speak of Christianity, let us, following the same principle, specify a particular aspect of the rich and various belief of the Church represented in the writings of the evangelists. That aspect, the common denominator of the Gospels, finds full expression in the simple claim that Jesus Christ died on the cross for our sins, rose from the dead, and so came to save humanity. Hence we shall center on a chapter in the salvific aspect of the Christianity represented by the Gospels (though not by them alone).

I maintain that we deal with different people talking about different things to different people for a simple reason. The Judaism defined by the system and method of the Pharisees addressed the issue of the sanctification of Israel, while Christianity as defined by the evangelists took up the question of the salvation of Israel. Both were expressions of biblical Israel's religion; one spoke of one thing, the other of something else. In retrospect, although they bear some traits in common, the two groups appear in no way comparable. Why not?

Take for example the definition of the system's social entity for example. Each appealed to a genus outside of the imagination of the other. The one spoke of family, the other of an inchoate group of people who obeyed rules in common. The Gospels portray the first Christians as the family and followers of Jesus. So, as a social group, Christianity represented at its outset in a quite physical, familial, and genealogical way "the body of Christ." The Pharisees, by contrast, hardly formed a special group at all. It is easier to say what they were not than what they were. How so? Although the Pharisees appear as a political group by the first century in Josephus's writings about Maccabean politics, the Gospels and the rabbinic traditions concur that what made an Israelite a Pharisee

---

[11]In fact, we deal with diverse groups talking to diverse audiences, a set of Judaic and Christian religious systems, respectively. How they form two distinct sets is not the problem of this paper.

was not exclusively or even mainly politics. The Pharisees were characterized by their adherence to certain cultic rules. They were not a member of a family in any natural or supernatural sense. Their social affiliations in no way proved homologous.

True, the Christians carried forward one aspect of Scripture's doctrine of Israel, and the Pharisees another. The Hebrew Scriptures represent Israel as one very large family, descended from a single set of ancestors. The Christians adopted that theory of Israel by linking themselves, first of all, to the family of Jesus and his adopted sons, the disciples, and secondly, through him and them to his ancestry – to David, and on backward to Abraham, Isaac, and Jacob (hence the enormous power of the genealogies of Christ.). The next step – the spiritualization of that familiar tie into the conception of the Church as the body of Christ – need not detain us. but Scripture did not restrict itself to the idea of Israel as family; it also defined Israel as a kingdom of priests and a holy people. That is the way taken by the Pharisees. Their Israel found commonality in a shared, holy way of life, required of all Israelites – so Scripture held. The Mosaic Torah defined that way of life in both cultic and moral terms, and the prophets laid great stress on the latter. What made Israel holy – its way of life, its moral character – depended primarily on how people lived, not upon their shared genealogy. Both Christians and Pharisees belonged to (an) "Israel"[12] but chose different definitions of the term. The Christians saw Israel as a family; the Pharisees saw it as a way of life. The Christians stressed their genealogy; the Pharisees their ethos and ethics. the Christian family held things in common; the holy people held in common a way of life that sanctified them. At issue in the argument between them are positions that scarcely intersect held by groups whose social self-definitions are incongruent.

Christianity and Judaism (as defined at the outset) each took over the inherited symbolic structure of Israel's religion. Each in fact did work with the same categories as the other. But, in the hands of each, the available and encompassing classification system found wholly new meaning. The upshot was two religions, each to be sure speaking within precisely the same categories, but so radically redefining the substance of these categories that conversation with the other became impossible. The similarity? Christ embodies God, just as the talmudic sage, or rabbi, in later times would be seen to stand for the torah incarnate.[13] The difference? Christ brought salvation, and, for the ages to come, the talmudic sage promised salvation. Salvation, in the nature of things, concerned the whole of humanity; sanctification, equally characteristic of its category, spoke of a single nation, Israel. To save, the messiah saves Israel amid all nations, because salvation categorically entails the eschatological

---

[12]I have expanded on this matter in my *"Israel." Judaism and its Social Metaphors* (New York and Cambridge: Cambridge University Press, 1988).

[13]I work on this comparison in my *Why No Gospels in Talmudic Judaism?* (Atlanta: Scholars Press for Brown Judaic Studies, 1987).

dimension, and so encompasses all of history. No salvation, after all, can last only for a little while, or leave space for time beyond itself. To sanctify, by contrast, the sage sanctifies Israel in particular. Sanctification categorically requires the designation of what is holy against what is not holy. To sanctify is to set apart. No sanctification can encompass everyone or leave no room for someone in particular to be holy. One need not be "holier than thou," but the *holy* requires the contrary category, the *not-holy*.

So, once more, how can two religious communities understand one another when one raises the issue of the sanctification of Israel, and the other the salvation of the world? Again, different people talking about different things to different people. Mutual comprehension becomes still more difficult when the familiar proves strange, when categories we think we understand we turn out not to grasp at all. Using the familiar in strange ways was, I maintain, the most formidable obstacle to resolving the Jewish-Christian argument in the first century. Both Christians and Pharisees radically revised existing categories. Each side took over the established classifications, but infused them with new meaning. Though in categories nothing changed, in substance nothing remained what it had been. That is why both Christian and Judaic thinkers reread the received Scriptures – "the Old Testament" to the one, "the Written Torah" to the other – and produced, respectively, "the New Testament" and the "Oral Torah."

When Jesus asked people who they thought he was, the enigmatic answer proved less interesting than the question posed. For the task, as portrayed by not only the Gospels but also Paul and the other New Testament writers, he set himself was to reframe everything people knew through encounter with what they did not know: a taxonomic enterprise. When the rabbis of late antiquity rewrote in their own image and likeness the entire Scripture and history of Israel, dropping whole eras as though they had never been, ignoring vast bodies of old Jewish writing, inventing whole new books for the canon of Judaism, they did the same thing. They reworked what they had received in light of what they proposed to give.

What then has proved to define the stakes in the insistence that to understand Christian scriptures, we need not merely inert facts but systemic statements that we identify as Judaic? As I see it, the urgency attached to that proposition derives from a positive and a negative motivation. The positive is the nurture of good will on the part of the majority religion toward the small and hated minority one. That accounts for the whole of the Jews' interest, and a considerable part of the Christians', in the appeal to Judaism for the solution of New Testament interpretive problems. But the other component of what is at stake has also to be recognized. It is wholly characteristic of Christian interest in the Judaic sources of Christianity. Since, as everyone knows, some earliest Christians were Jews and saw their religion as normative and authoritative; (a) Judaism, a natural question troubling believing Christians is why Judaism as a whole remains a religion that believes other things, or, as Christians commonly ask, "Why did the Jews not 'accept Christ'?" or "Why, after the resurrection of Jesus Christ, is there Judaism at all?"

Often asked negatively, the question turns on why the Jews do not believe, rather than on what they do believe. The upshot is that there really is no interest at all in "Judaism" in any form, except for precisely the same reason that the earlier Christians, no longer "the old Israel" in their own estimation, took an interest in that "Judaism" that they claimed to confront. It is simply part of the systemic statement of Christianity to address Judaism with the question: Why not? For the asking of the question – "Why not?" rather than "Why so?" – reflects the long-term difficulty that the one group has had in making sense of the other. Responding by appeal to the nature and condition of Judaism has yielded those invidious comparisons, for instance, between legalistic Judaism and moral Christianity, that Christians of good will these days ordinarily set aside. But the reading of the portrait of Judaism composed by Christianity, absolute and utterly different from all else, as an account of how things were, that is, as a picture of a Judaic system, remains as a legacy. We now understand that in the literature called *adversus judaeos*, Justin's Trypho, Aphrahat's "sage," or "debater of the people," and the like, form Christian inventions for the purposes of disputation. And so too does that Judaism that forms an urgent systemic component of diverse Christian authorships, indeed, not merely constituent but a compulsion. But that invented, essentially fictive Judaism tells us only about the system-builders who invented it. That is why, I should suggest, in the interpretation of the New Testament and the formative centuries of Christianity, salvation is really not of the Jews, not at all.

Chapter Nine

Bavli *versus* Bible:
System and Imputed Tradition *versus* Tradition and Imputed System

Once we recognize that two sets of religious systems differ from one another, then we may begin the work of interpretation through comparison and contrast. And in the study of the history of Judaism, the ineluctable source of comparisons derives from Christianity, because all Judaic and Christian systems appeal to the same original Scripture, the Written Torah for the Judaism of the dual Torah, which is the same as the Old Testament for all Orthodox and Catholic Christianity. They commonly do so, moreover, in pretty much the same way, that is to say, by quoting verses of ancient Israel's Scripture as proof-texts for propositions. Implicit is the same position, that the (selected) Scripture of ancient Israel bore probative authority in disposing of claims of the faith.[1] And that simple fact further defines the point of comparison. To specify what I deem comparable in the two traditions, I point to the simple fact that each defines its authority by appeal to revelation, and both religious traditions know precisely the locus of revelation. Christianity finds in the Bible, meaning the Old Testament and the New Testament, the statement of the faith by the authority of God.[2] Judaism from antiquity to our own day has identified in the Bavli, the Talmud of Babylonia, the summa of the Torah of Sinai, joining as it does the Written Torah, encompassing what Christianity knows as the Old Testament, and the Oral Torah, commencing with the Mishnah. The Bible, for Christianity, and the Bavli, for Judaism, have formed the court of final appeal in

---

[1]The Islamic appeal to the Old Testament/written Torah requires attention in its own terms. I am not qualified to undertake the comparison of the use of that ancient scripture in the Quran and later Islamic writings or to suggest how that use compares with, and contrasts to, the Judaic and Christian use of the same writings. In this respect, however, I do think there really is a "Judeo-Christian" tradition, but it is, of course, one that divides, and not unites, the Judaic and Christian religions.

[2]It is not pertinent to deal with *tradition* as a correlative source of God's truth, and I take no position on controverted issues of theology of Christianity as to whether solely Scripture, or also Scripture and tradition preserved by the teaching authority of the Church, constitute the authoritative repository of revelation.

issues of doctrine and (for Judaism) normative instruction on correct deed as well. Commentaries, paraphrases, amplifications have carried out that exegetical elaboration that spun out a web of relationships. The pattern of truth that, for the Bible and for the Bavli alike, served to state the world view and way of life for Church and "Israel," respectively, furthermore was endowed with the status of revealed truth and to the ethos and ethics of the social entity was imputed the standing of tradition.

But, while the comparison is not only justified but demanded, still, the Bavli and the Bible are quite different kinds of documents. And in the differences we see the choices people made when confronting pretty much the same problem. For, in late antiquity, from the second through the fourth centuries for Orthodox, Catholic Christianity, and from the second through the seventh centuries for the Judaism of the dual Torah, the Judaic and Christian intellectuals sorted out the complex problem of relating the worlds of the then-moderns to the words of the ancients. Both groups of intellectuals then claimed to present enduring traditions, a fundament of truth revealed of old. But both sets of thinkers also brought to realization systematic and philosophical statements, which begin in first principles and rise in steady and inexorable logic to final conclusions: compositions of proportion, balance, cogency, and order.

In the case of the Jewish mind represented by the intellects of the dual Torah, the system came in three parts, the Pentateuch, the Mishnah, and, in the present context, the Bavli.[3] A simple question then faced the heirs of the Pentateuch (and the rest of the Hebrew Scriptures) as well as the Mishnah and the body of Mishnah interpretation produced between 200 and ca. 400 (for the Land of Israel) and ca. 600 (for Babylonia). How to relate the three systems? It was by forming the final statement that the Bavli's authorship wished to make into the form of a commentary on the Mishnah and on Scripture alike. True, the "commentary" that bore the burden of the Bavli's system would address only those passages that the authorship of the Bavli found consequential. But that independent act of selectivity formed a principal intellectual labor of system-building.

---

[3]Much that is said here can be said also of the Yerushalmi. But I should claim that the authorships of Leviticus Rabbah, Genesis Rabbah, Pesiqta deRab Kahana, and other compilations of thought set forth in close relationship to the written Torah, had also to think through the same problem of the relationship of received truth to the autonomous thought of a well-composed system. What I say of the Bavli's authorship's intellect pertains to the other authorships within the canon of the Judaism of the dual Torah as it reached conclusion in late antiquity. But I readily admit that each authorship has to be read in its own documentary setting, and only at the end of that considerable process can the generalizations offered here, resting on what I see as the Bavli's authorship's solution to the shared problem of sorting out the interplay of system and tradition, be refined and correctly restated to cover the whole of the canon.

What makes the formation of the Bavli interesting is the parallel problem facing Christian theologians in the same age. In the case of the Christian mind, where do we look for a counterpart labor of system-building through selectivity? The answer, of course, is dictated by the form of the question. We turn to the work of canonization of available writings into the Bible. There we see the theologians' work of the making of choices, the setting forth of a single statement. When we compare the systemic structures represented by the Bavli and the Bible, therefore, we can appreciate how two quite distinct groups of intellectuals worked out solutions to a single problem, and did so, as a matter of fact, through pretty much the same medium, namely, the making of reasoned choices. Both authorships set forth systems of thought, at the same time attaching to their systems the claim of tradition: God's Torah to Moses at Sinai, for Judaism, the pattern of Christian truth, for Christianity, hence the comparison of Bavli and Bible.

But then the points of difference are determined by the shared morphology: the Bible and the Bavli are very different ways of setting forth a system. Each represents its components in a distinctive manner, the one by preserving their autonomy and calling the whole a system, the other by obscuring their originally autonomous and independent character and imparting to the whole the form of tradition. The upshot may be simply stated. The Bavli presents a system and to it through the operative logics imputes the standing of tradition. The Bible sets forth diverse and unsystematic traditions, received writings from we know not where, and to those traditions, through the act of canonization, imputes the character and structure of (a) system.

To unpack these generalizations, let us turn back to the literary media in which the intellects of the two communities of intellectuals set forth their system as traditions or their traditions as system: the Bavli and the Bible, respectively. We wish specifically to see how each of these monuments of mind works out its own system and, consequently, also, accomplishes the resulting tasks at hand, first, the sorting out of the issue of choosing a logic of cogent discourse to serve the interests of the system, second, the situating of the system in relationship to received and authoritative, prior systemic statements.

In the case of the Bavli, our point of entry is the identification of the odd mixture of logics utilized by the framers of the system as a whole. When we understand the character of the Mishnah and its relationship to the immediately prior system its authorship recognized, which was the Pentateuch (and Scripture as a whole), we shall grasp the choices confronting the Bavli's framers. The issue presented by the Mishnah, which the Bavli in its form is arranged to serve as a vast exegesis, derives from the form and character of the Mishnah itself. For the Mishnah utilized a single logic to set forth a system that, in form as in inner structure, stood wholly autonomous and independent, a statement unto itself, with scarcely a ritual obeisance to any prior system. As soon as the Mishnah made its appearance, therefore, the vast labor of not only explaining its meaning but especially justifying its authority was sure to get under way. For the Mishnah presented one striking problem in particular. It rarely cited scriptural authority for its rules. Instead, it followed the inexorable authority of logic, specifically, the inner logic of a topic, which dictated the order of thought and defined the generative problematic that instructed its authors on what they wanted to know about a particular topic.[4] These intellectual modalities in their nature lay claim to an independence of mind, even when, in point of fact, the result of thought is a repetition of what Scripture itself says. Omitting scriptural proof texts therefore represents both silence and signals its statement. For that act of omission bore the implicit claim to an authority independent of Scripture, an authority deriving from logic working within its own inner tensions and appealing to tests of reason and sound argument. In that striking fact the document set a new course for itself. But its authorship raised problems for those who would apply its law to Israel's life.

For from the formation of ancient Israelite Scripture into a holy book in Judaism, in the aftermath of the return to Zion and the creation of the Torah-book in Ezra's time (ca. 450 B.C.) the established canon of revelation (whatever its contents) coming generations routinely set their ideas into relationship with Scripture. This they did by citing proof-texts alongside their own rules. Otherwise, in the setting of Israelite culture, the new writings could find no ready hearing. Over the six hundred years from the formation of the Torah of "Moses" in the time of Ezra, from ca. 450 B.C. to ca. A.D. 200, four conventional ways to accommodate new writings – new "tradition" – to the established canon of received Scripture had come to the fore. First and simplest, a writer would sign a famous name to his book, attributing his ideas to Enoch, Adam, Jacob's sons, Jeremiah, Baruch, and any number of others, down to Ezra. But the Mishnah bore no such attribution, e.g., to Moses. Implicitly, to be sure, the statement of M. Avot 1:1, "Moses received Torah from Sinai" carried the further notion that sayings of people on the list of authorities from Moses to nearly their own day derived from God's revelation at Sinai. But no one made that premise explicit before the time of the Bavli of the Land of Israel. Second, an authorship might also imitate the style of biblical Hebrew and so try to creep into the canon by adopting the cloak of Scripture. But the Mishnah's authorship ignores biblical syntax and style. Third, an author would surely claim his work was inspired by God, a new revelation for an open canon. But, as we realize, that claim makes no explicit impact on the Mishnah. Fourth, at the very least,

---

[4]I have spelled these matters out for the second through the sixth divisions of the Mishnah in my *History of the Mishnaic Law* (Leiden: E. J. Brill, 1974-1985) in forty-three volumes. For each tractate I show how the topic at hand was analyzed by the tractate's framers, proving that what they identified as the problematic of the topic instructed those writers on what they wanted to know about the topic and also on the correct, logical order in which they would state the results of their inquiry.

someone would link his opinions to biblical verses through the exegesis of the latter in line with the former so Scripture would validate his views. The authorship of the Mishnah did so only occasionally, but far more commonly stated on its own authority whatever rules it proposed to lay down.

The Hebrew of the Mishnah complicated the problem, because it is totally different from the Hebrew of the Hebrew Scriptures. Its verb, for instance, makes provision for more than completed or continuing action, for which the biblical Hebrew verb allows, but also for past and future times, subjunctive and indicative voices, and much else. The syntax is Indo-European, in that we can translate the word order of the Mishnah into any Indo-European language and come up with perfect sense. None of that crabbed imitation of biblical Hebrew, that makes the Dead Sea scrolls an embarassment to read, characterizes the Hebrew of the Mishnah. Mishnaic style is elegant, subtle, exquisite in its sensitivity to word order and repetition, balance, pattern.

The solution to the problem of the authority of the Mishnah, that is to say, its relationship to Scripture, was worked out in the period after the closure of the Mishnah. Since no one now could credibly claim to sign the name of Ezra or Adam to a book of this kind, and since biblical Hebrew had provided no apologetic aesthetics whatever, the only options lay elsewhere. The two were, first, to provide a myth of the origin of the contents of the Mishnah, and, second, to link each allegation of the Mishnah, through processes of biblical (not Mishnaic) exegesis, to verses of the Scriptures. These two procedures, together, would establish for the Mishnah that standing that the uses to which the document was to be put demanded for it: a place in the canon of Israel, a legitimate relationship to the Torah of Moses. There were several ways in which the work went forward. These are represented by diverse documents that succeeded and dealt with the Mishnah. Let me now state the three principal possibilities. (1) The Mishnah required no systematic support through exegesis of Scripture in light of Mishnaic laws. (2) The Mishnah by itself provided no reliable information and all of its propositions demanded linkage to Scripture, to which the Mishnah must be shown to be subordinate and secondary. (3) The Mishnah is an autonomous document, but closely correlated with Scripture.

The first extreme is represented by the Avot, ca. 250 A.D., which represents the authority of the sages cited in Avot as autonomous of Scripture. Those authorities in Avot do not cite verses of Scripture but what they say does constitute a statement of the Torah. There can be no clearer way of saying that what these authorities present in and of itself falls into the classification of the Torah. The authorship of the Tosefta, ca. 400 A.D., takes the middle position. It very commonly cites a passage of the Mishnah and then adds to that passage an appropriate proof-text. That is a quite common mode of supplementing the Mishnah. The mediating view is further taken by the Yerushalmi and the Bavli, ca. 400-600. With the Yerushalmi's authorship, that of the Bavli developed a well-crafted theory of the Mishnah and its relationship to Scripture. Each rule of the Mishnah is commonly introduced, in the exegesis supplied by the two Talmuds, with the question, "What is the source of this statement?" And the answer invariably is, "As it is said," or "... written," with a verse of Scripture, that is, the Written Torah, then cited. The upshot is that the source of the rules of the Mishnah (and other writings) is Scripture, not free-standing logic. The far extreme – everything in the Mishnah makes sense only as a (re)statement of Scripture or upon Scripture's authority – is taken by the Sifra, a post-Mishnaic compilation of exegeses on Leviticus, redacted at an indeterminate point, perhaps about 300 A.D. The Sifra systematically challenges reason (that is, the Mishnah), unaided by revelation (that is, exegesis of Scripture), to sustain positions taken by the Mishnah, which is cited verbatim, and everywhere proves that it cannot be done.

The final and normative solution to the problem of the authority of the Mishnah worked out in the third and fourth centuries produced the myth of the dual Torah, oral and written, which formed the indicative and definitive trait of the Judaism that emerged from late antiquity. Tracing the unfolding of that myth leads us deep into the processes by which that Judaism took shape. The Bavli knows the theory that there is a tradition separate from, and in addition to, the Written Torah. This tradition it knows as "the teachings of scribes." The Mishnah is identified as the collection of those teachings only by implication in the Bavli. I cannot point to a single passage in which explicit judgment upon the character and status of the Mishnah as a complete document is laid down. Nor is the Mishnah treated as a symbol or called "the Oral Torah." But there is ample evidence, once again implicit in what happens to the Mishnah in the Bavli, to allow a reliable description of how the Bavli's founders viewed the Mishnah. That view may be stated very simply. The Mishnah rarely cites verses of Scripture in support of its propositions. The Bavli routinely adduces Scriptural bases for the Mishnah's laws. The Mishnah seldom undertakes the exegesis of verses of Scripture for any purpose. The Bavli consistently investigates the meaning of verses of Scripture, and does so for a variety of purposes. Accordingly, the Bavli, subordinate as it is to the Mishnah, regards the Mishnah as subordinate to, and contingent upon, Scripture. That is why, in the Bavli's view, the Mishnah requires the support of proof-texts of Scripture. By itself, the Mishnah exercises no autonomous authority and enjoys no independent standing or norm-setting status.

Now this brings us back, by a circuitous route, to the Bavli's authorship's explanation of its own position in relationship to the received "tradition," which is to say, to prior systemic statements, the Pentateuch's and the Mishnah's in particular. Their solution to the problem of the standing and authority of the Mishnah dictated their answer to the question of the representation, within a received tradition, of their own system as well. It was through phrase by phrase commentary that the Bavli's authorship justified the Mishnah as tradition and represented it as a secondary elaboration of Scripture or as invariably resting on the authority of Scripture. That form, as we realize, does what can be done to represent sentences of the Mishnah as related to sentences of Scripture. That mode of writing, moreover, accomplished what we may call the dismantling or deconstruction of the system of the Mishnah and the reconstruction of its bits and pieces into the system of the Bavli. For, as even the little sample in the preceding chapter has shown us, the Bavli's authorship never represented the Mishnah's system whole and complete, and rarely acknowledged that the Mishnah consisted of more than discrete statements, to be related to some larger cogent law that transcended the Mishnah.[5]

Having represented the Mishnah as it did, the Bavli's authorship quite naturally chose to represent its own system in the same way, that is to say, as a mere elaboration of a received tradition, a stage in the sedimentary and incremental process by which the Torah continued to come down from Sinai. And for that purpose, I hardly need to add, the mixed logics embodied in the joining of philosophical and propositional statements on the principle of fixed association – commentary attached to a prior text – served exceedingly well. That explains how, in the Bavli, we have, in the (deceptive) form of a tradition, what is in fact an autonomous system, connected with prior systems but not continuous with them. The authorship represented their own statement of an ethos, ethics, and defined social entity, precisely as they did the received ones, the whole forming a single, seamless Torah revealed by God to Moses at Sinai.[6]

---

[5]The identification of this transcendent system that is implicit in the intellect of the Bavli's system-builders requires study on its own. I cannot claim to know its composition and components.

[6]And that further explains why the Bavli's authorship encompassed within their statement vast tracts of other rabbinic compilations now known to us, e.g., the Tosefta, Sifra, Sifré to Numbers and the one to Deuteronomy, Genesis Rabbah, and so on and so forth. By contrast, the representation in a given document of materials particular to another document is hardly common. And when an authorship or group of collectors and arrangers, such as that of Pesiqta deRab Kahana, does make use of materials that occur in another compilation altogether, they do not then revise and impose their own distinctive traits of formalization and expression upon the received writing. This I have shown for the chapters of Pesiqta deRab Kahana that occur, also, in Leviticus Rabbah. In the case of all five of them, the indicative literary traits accord with those prevailing in Leviticus Rabbah and differ from those characteristic of the chapters of Pesiqta deRab Kahana that are not shared with Leviticus Rabbah. I have the impression that the same result can be produced for shared items in other compilations as well. But that applies, specifically, to large-scale compositions. As to singleton sayings, little formulas, phrases, and the like, these may appear hither and yon. They are too small, so far as I can see, to be reshaped in terms of the large-scale and systematic literary program of the framers of whole documents, so constitute, from a form-analytical viewpoint, systemically inert entries. That is how a saying can float about without being reshaped in any material way for the purposes of an authorship that makes use of it, while a sizable composition, something we would (anachronistically) call a set of three or four continuous paragraphs, will be

So much for a system to which the standing of tradition is imputed through formal means.

When we come to the counterpart religious world, we confront Christian intellectuals, dealing also with the inheritance of ancient Israel's scriptures facing the same problem. The parallel is exact in yet another aspect. Just as the authorship of the Bavli received not only what they came to call the Written Torah, but also the Mishnah and other writings that had attained acceptance, hence authority, from the closure of the Mishnah to their own day, so too did the Christian intellectuals inherit more than the Old Testament. They too had in hand a variety of authoritative documents, to which the inspiration of the Holy Spirit was imputed. So they confronted the same problem as faced the authorship of the Bavli, and it was in pretty much the same terms: namely, how to sort out received documents, each of which making its own statement[7] take up a different problem and follow a different solution to that problem.

What they did was to join together the received writings as autonomous books but to impute to the whole the standing of a single, coherent and cogent statement, a harmonious Christian truth. This they did in the work of making the biblical canon,[8] joining diverse traditions into one, single, uniform, and,

---

revised in terms of the documentary traits of form and structure for insertion into that document. This too is a subject warranting attention in its own terms and need not detain us for the argument of this chapter.

[7]Whether that is a systemic statement or not, and for the present purpose, the analysis of systemic compositions and constructions within the Christian framework is not required. My purpose is solely to place into relationship two solutions to the problem of system and tradition. While an analysis of the systemic traits of Christian writings down to the canonization of the (Christian) Bible (the Old Testament and the New Testament) in my judgment would prove exceedingly suggestive, it has not been done, and I cannot pretend to be able to do it. As is clear, I conceive the Bible to represent a solution to a problem of the same order as that solved, through the formal including the logical traits of the Bavli, by the Bavli's authorship. But beyond that point, I cannot go, e.g., I cannot judge whether or not we find Christian systems only in Irenaeus, Origen, and Augustine, as seems to me the case, or also in other writings, circles, documents, and the like; whether or not theology, in Christianity, forms a counterpart to the system building that yielded the Mishnah, the Yerushalmi, the Bavli, and other writings in the Judaism of the dual Torah, and so on and so forth. I owe to my colleague, Wendell S. Dietrich, the asking of those tough questions that made me realize the limitations of the proposals presented here.

[8]I hasten to add, they did so not only in the process of the canonization of some writings as the Old Testament and the New Testament, the Bible. It seems to me the work of framing creeds, preparing liturgies to be used throughout the church(es), debating theology and the like, all attended to the same labor of stating the pattern of Christian truth out of the received writings, all of them claiming to derive from the Holy Spirit or to be consonant with writings that did, that competed for standing and that contradicted one another on pretty much every important point. Once more, I underline that in dealing only with the work of

therefore, (putatively) harmonious Bible: God's word. And, once more, that explains my view that the Christian solution to the problem of making a statement but also situating that system in relationship to received tradition is to be characterized as imputing system to discrete traditions through a declared canon. Thus, as in the title of this chapter, the comparison of the solutions that would prevail, respectively, in Judaism's Bavli and Christianity's Bible, are characterized as a system to which the standing of tradition is imputed, as against traditions, to which the form of a single system is, through the canonization of scriptures as the Bible, imputed.[9] The legitimacy of my comparing the two intellects through their ultimate statements, the Bavli and the Bible, seems to me sustained by the simple theological judgment of Turner:

> The mind of the Church [in making the canon] was guided by criteria rationally devised and flexibly applied. There is no dead hand in the production of the Canon; there is rather the living action of the Holy Spirit using as He is wont the full range of the continuing life of the Church to achieve His purposes in due season.[10]

I can find no better language to state, in a way interior to a system, the claim that a writing or a set of writings constitutes a system: a way of life, a world view, an address to a particular social entity. This too is made explicit by Turner, who I take to be a thoroughly reliable representative of Christian theology on the subject:

> There can be no doubt that the Bible is fundamentally an orthodox book, sufficient if its teaching is studied as a whole to lead to orthodox conclusions .... The Biblical data insist upon arranging themselves in certain theological patterns and cannot be forced into other moulds without violent distortion. That is the point of a famous simile of St. Irenaeus. The teaching of Scripture can be compared to a mosaic of the head of a king, but the heretics break up the pattern and reassemble it in the form of a dog or a fox.[11]

A master of the Bavli could not have said it better in claiming both the systemic character, and the traditional standing, of his statement.

---

canon, I in no way pretend to address the broader issues implicit in the topic as I have defined it.

[9]In laying matters out, I avoid entering the issues debated by Walter Bauer, *Orthodoxy and Heresy in Earliest Christianity* (Philadelphia: Fortress, 1971), translation of *Rechtgläubigkeit und Ketzerei im ältesten Christentum* (1934, supplemented by Georg Strecker, 1964), edited by Robert A. Kraft and Gerhard Krodel, and H. E. W. Turner, *The Pattern of Christian Truth. A Study of the Relations between Orthodoxy and Heresy in the Early Church. Bampton Lectures, 1954* (London: A. R. Mowbray & Co., Ltd., 1954). I do claim that my representation of matters accords with Turner's chapter, "Orthodoxy and the Bible," pp. 241ff.

[10]Turner, p. 258.

[11]Turner, p. 300.

Let me hasten to qualify the comparison at hand. In claiming that a single problem, one of relating a system to tradition, for Judaism, or traditions into a system, for Christianity, found two solutions in the Bavli and the Bible, respectively, I do not for one minute suggest that the two groups of intellectuals were thinking along the same lines at all. Quite to the contrary, the comparison derives from a different standpoint altogether. For, if we ask, when the Christian theologians worked out the idea of "the Bible," consisting of "the Old Testament and the New Testament," and when the Judaic theologians worked out the idea of "the dual Torah," consisting of "the Written Torah and the Oral Torah," did each group propose to answer a question confronting the other group as well? We answer negative. For, as a matter of fact, each party pursued a problem particular to the internal logic and life of its own group. True, as a matter of necessity, each party had to designate within the larger corpus of scriptures deriving from ancient Israel those writings that it regarded as authoritative, therefore divinely revealed. But did the one side do so for the same reasons, and within the same sort of theological logic, that the other did? Each party had further to explain to itself the end result, that is, the revealed words as a whole? What are they all together, all at once? The one party characterized the whole as a single Bible, book, piece of writing, and the other party characterized the whole as a single Torah, revelation, in two media, the one, writing, the other, memory. But these characterizations of the result of revelation, that is, of the canon, hardly constitute intersecting statements.

The reason that, for Christianity, traditions became a system, as Turner testifies, was the intent and the outcome, derives from the life of the Church, not from the issue of culture in its relationship to the logic of cogent discourse that I have framed here. Let us briefly review the formation of the received, that is, traditional writings into a system, that is, as Turner says, a canon, a pattern of Christian truth. In the centuries after the Gospels were written, the Church had to come to a decision on whether, in addition to the Scriptures of ancient Israel, there would be a further corpus of authoritative writing. The Church affirmed that there would be, and the New Testament as counterpart to the Old Testament evolved into the canon. When we speak of canon, we refer, in Childs's words, to "the process of theological interpretation by a faith community [that] left its mark on a literary text which did not continue to evolve and which became the normative interpretation of the events to which it bore witness for those identifying with that religious community."[12]

Christians from the very beginning revered the Hebrew Scriptures as "the Old Testament," regarding it as their sacred book. They denied the Jews any claim to the book, accusing them of misinterpreting it. The Old Testament served, in Harnack's words, to prove "that the appearance and the entire history of Jesus had been predicted hundreds and even thousands of years ago; and further,

---

[12]Childs, Brevard S., *The New Testament as Canon*, p. 26.

that the founding of the New People which was to be fashioned out of all the nations upon earth had from the very beginning been prophesied and prepared for." The text of the Hebrew Scriptures supplied proofs for various propositions of theology, law, and liturgy. It served as a source of precedents: "If God had praised or punished this or that in the past, how much more ... are we to look for similar treatment from him, we who are now living in the last days and who have received 'the calling of promise.'" Even after the rise of the New Testament, much of the Old Testament held its own. And, Harnack concludes, "The New Testament as a whole did not generally play the same role as the Old Testament in the mission and practice of the church."[13]

In the beginning the Church did not expect the canon – now meaning only the Hebrew Scripture – to grow through Christian additions. As Cross says, "In the new covenant the sole complement to the Word in the Torah was the Word made flesh in Christ." So it would be some time before a Christian canon encompassing not only the received writings but the writings of the new age would come into being. For, until the time at hand, the Bible of the Church consisted of the Hebrew Scriptures, "the Old Testament." Before Marcion the Bible of the Church was the Hebrew Scriptures, pure and simple. While Filson assigns to the years between 160 and 175 the crystallization of the concept of the canon, the process came to the end by the end of the fourth century. Filson states, "There was no longer any wide dispute over the right of any of our twenty-seven books to a place in the New Testament canon." What was not a settled question for Eusebius, in 330, had been worked out in the next span of time. So, in general, when we take up the issue of the canon of Christianity, we find ourselves in the third and fourth centuries.[14] The bulk of the work was complete by 200, with details under debate for another two hundred years.[15] The orthodoxy in which "the canon of an Old and a New Testament was firmly laid down," did not come into being overnight. From the time of Irenaeus the church affirmed the bipartite Christian Bible, containing the Old, and, parallel with this and controlling it, the New Testament.[16] But what was to be in the New Testament, and when were the limits of the canon decided? Von Campenhausen concludes the description for us:

> [The Muratorian fragment] displays for the first time the concept of a collection of New Testament scriptures, which has deliberately been closed, and the individual books of which are regarded as "accepted" and eccleisastically "sanctified," that is to say ... they have been "incorporated" into the valid corpus. We have thus arrived at the end of the long journey which leads to a New Testament thought of as "canonical" in the strict sense. Only one thing is still lacking: the

---

[13] Harnack, Adolf, *Mission and Expansion of Christianity*, pp. 283-4.
[14] Cross, p. 60, von Campenhausen, p. 147, Filson, p. 121.
[15] Childs, p. 18.
[16] Von Campenhausen, p. 209.

precise name for this collection, which will make it possible to refer to the new Scripture as a unity and thus at one and the same time both to distinguish it from the old Scriptures and combine it with them in a new totality .... This is the last feature still wanting to the accomplishment of the bipartite Christian Bible.[17]

When does the Old Testament join the New as the Bible? Von Campenhausen makes a striking point. There was no need to look for a single name for the entire document. There was no such thing as an Old Testament or a New Testament as a single physical entity. To the eye the whole canon was still fragmented into a series of separate rolls or volumes. Von Campenhausen makes a still more relevant point:

There was no reason why in themselves the two parts of the Bible should not have different names. In the early period one possibility suggested itself almost automatically: if one had the New and the Old Testament in mind, one could speak of the 'Gospel' and the 'Law.'[18]

The use of "Old" and "New" Testament represents a particular theology. It was from the beginning of the third century that Scripture for orthodox Christianity consisted of an Old and a New Testament. So, we conclude, "Both the Old and the New Testaments had in essence already reached their final form and significance around the year 200."[19] The authority of the Bible, for Christianity, rested on the reliability of the biblical record of, the predictions of Christ in the prophets and the testimony to Christ of the apostles.[20] The biblical component of the "canon of truth" proved contingent, not absolute and dominant.

We now realize that the issues important to the Judaism of the sages were in no way consubstantial, let alone comparable, with the issues at hand. None of the cited theological precipitants for the canonical process in a Judaic formulation played any role I can discern in the theory of the Torah in two media. The myth of the dual Torah, which functioned as a canonical process, validating as it did the writings of sages as part of Torah from Sinai, derives from neither the analogy to the Old Testament process nor – to begin with – from the narrow issue of finding a place for the specific writings of rabbis within the larger Torah, and, it follows, *we cannot refer to "the Bible" when we speak of Judaism.*

When scholars of the formation of the canon of Christianity use the word canon, they mean, first, the recognition of sacred Scripture, over and beyond the (received) Hebrew Scriptures, second, the identification of writings revered within the Church as canonical, hence authoritative, third, the recognition that these

[17]Von Campenhausen, pp. 261-262.
[18]Von Campenhausen, p. 262. Cf. also p. 261-2.
[19]Von Campenhausen, p. 327.
[20]*Idem.*, p. 330.

accepted writings formed a Scripture, which, fourth, served as the counterpart to the Hebrew Scriptures, hence, fifth, the formation of the Bible as the Old and New Testaments. Now, as a matter of fact, none of these categories, stage by stage, corresponds in any way to the processes in the unfolding of the holy books of the sages, which I shall now describe in terms of Torah. But the word "Torah" in the context of the writings of the sages at hand in no way forms that counterpart to the word "canon" as used (quite correctly) by Childs, von Campenhausen, and others, and, moreover the word "Bible" and the word "Torah" in no way speak of the same thing, I mean, they do not refer to the same category or classification.

In fact the statement of the Bavli is not a canonical system at all. For in the mode of presentation of the Bavli's system, as a matter of fact, revelation does not close or reach conclusion. God speaks all the time, through the sages. Representing the whole as "Torah" means that the Bavli speaks a tradition formed in God's revelation of God's will to Moses, our rabbi. Ancient Israel's scriptures fall into the category of Torah, but they do not fill that category up. Other writings fall into that same category. By contrast canon refers to particular books that enjoy a distinctive standing, Torah refers to various things that fall into a particular classification. The Christian canon reached closure with the Bible: Old and New Testaments. The Judaic Torah never closed: revelation of Torah continued.[21] The Torah is not the Bible, and the Bible is not the Torah. The Bible emerges from the larger process of establishing Church order and doctrine.[22] The Torah ("Oral and Written") for its part derives from the larger process of working out in relationship to the Pentateuchal system the authority and standing of two successive and connected systems that had followed, the Mishnah, then the Bavli.

A long-standing problem faced all system-builders in the tradition that commenced with the Pentateuch. From that original system onward, system-builders, both in Judaism and, as we now realize, in Christianity, would have to represent their system not as an original statement on its own, but as part of a tradition of revealed truth. Not only so, but in the passage of time and in the accumulation of writing, intellectuals, both Christian and Judaic, would have to work out logics that would permit cogent discourse within the inherited traditions and with them. In the Christian case, the solution to the problem lay in accepting as canonical a variety of documents, each with its own logic. We

---

[21]So too did the pattern of Christian truth, but in a different form and forum from the canonical Bible.

[22]I cannot pretend to know whether or not von Campenhausen's arguments about the emergence of the New Testament in response to Montanism prove valid. I can flatly state that the issue – providing a basis to sort out the claims of living prophets, with direct access to divine teachings – bears no point of intersection – let alone comparison and contrast – with anything known to me in the entire corpus of rabbinic writing of late antiquity.

note, for instance, that extraordinarily cogent communication could be accomplished, in some Christian writings, through symbol and not through proposition at all. Christian writings exhibit each its own coherent logical principles of cogency, with the making of connections and the drawing of conclusions fully consistent throughout.

The final solution of the canon side-stepped the problem of bringing these logics together within a single statement. If diverse logics work, each for its own authoritative writing, then I do not have to effect coherence among diverse logics at all, and the canon, the conception of The Bible, would impose from without a cogency of discourse difficult to discern in the interior of the canonical writings. That decision would then dictate the future of the Christian intellectual enterprise: to explore the underbrush of the received writing and to straighten out the tangled roots. No wonder, then, that, in philosophy, culminating in the return to Athens, the Christian mind would recover that glory of logical and systematic order denied it in the dictated canon, the Bible. But the canon did solve the problem that faced the heirs to a rather odd corpus of writing. Ignoring logic as of no account, accepting considerable diversity in modes of making connections and drawing conclusions, the traditional solution represented a better answer than the librarians of the Essenes at Qumran had found, which was to set forth (so far as matters now seem at any rate) neither a system nor a canon.

The Bavli's authorship was the first in the history of Judaism, encompassing Christianity in its earliest phases,[23] to take up, in behalf of its distinct and distinctive system, a position of relationship with the received heritage of tradition, with a corpus of truth assigned to God's revelation to Moses at Sinai. The framers of the Pentateuch did not do so; rather they said what they wrote was the work of God, dictating to Moses at Sinai. The Essene librarians at Qumran did not do so. They collected this and that, never even pretending that everything fit together in some one way, not as commentary to Scripture (though some wrote commentaries), not as systemic statements (though the library included such statements, as we noticed), and not as a canon (unless everything we find in the detritus forms a canon by definition). The authorship of the Mishnah did not do so. Quite to the contrary, it undertook the pretense that, even when Scripture supplied facts and even dictated the order of the facts, their writing was new and fresh and their own.[24] No wonder that the

---

[23]I do not mean to ignore the school of Matthew and the numerous other Christian writers who cited proof-texts for their propositions. But as in the case of their Judaic counterparts, merely citing proof-texts is not the same thing as setting forth a complete *system* in the form of a *tradition,* such as was done by the Bavli's authorship.

[24]The best example is Mishnah tractate Yoma, Chapters One through Seven, which sedulously follow the order of Leviticus 16 and reviews its rite, step by step, rarely citing the pertinent chapter of Scripture and never conceding that all that was in hand was a summary and paraphrase of rules available elsewhere. It is the simple fact that we cannot make any sense out of that tractate without a point-

Mishnah's authorship resorted to its own logic to make its own statement in its own language and for its own purposes. No wonder, too, that the hubris of the Mishnah's authorship provoked the systematic demonstration of the dependence of the Mishnah on Scripture – but also the allegation that the Mishnah stood as an autonomous statement, another Torah, the oral one, coequal with the Written Torah. The hubris of the great intellects of Judaic and Christian antiquity, the daring authorships of the Pentateuch and the Mishnah, the great ecclesiastical minds behind the Bible, reached its boldest realization in the Bavli. This authorship accomplished, as we have seen, through its ingenious joining of two distinct and contradictory logics of cogent discourse the statement of the Torah in its own rhetoric, following its own logic, and in accord with its own designated topical program. But hubris is not the sole trait that characterizes the Jewish mind, encompassing its Christian successors, in classical times.

There is a second trait common to them all. It is that in all systemic constructions and statements the issues of logic responded to the systemic imperative and in no way dictated the shape and structure of that imperative. The system invariably proves to be prior, recapitulating itself, also, in its logic. And however diverse the issues addressed by various systems made up by the Jewish mind in classical times, all had to address a single question natural to the religious ecology in which Judaic systems flourished. That question, in the aftermath of the Pentateuchal system, concerned how people could put together in a fresh construction and a composition of distinctive proportions a statement that purported to speak truth to a social entity that, in the nature of things, already had truth. This framing of the issue of how system contradicts tradition, how the logic that tells me to make a connection of this to that, but not to the other thing, and to draw from that connection one conclusion, rather than some other – that framing of the issue places intellect, the formation of mind and modes of thought squarely into the ongoing processes dictated by the givens of society.

Why then characterize the Bavli's system-builders as the climax of the hubris of the Jewish intellectuals? Because the Bavli's authorship was the first in the history of Judaism, encompassing Christianity in its earliest phases, to take up, in behalf of its distinct and distinctive system, a position of relationship with the received heritage of tradition, with a corpus of truth assigned to God's revelation to Moses at Sinai. Prior systems had stood on their own, beginning, after all, with that of the Pentateuch itself in ca. 450 B.C. Four centuries after the Mishnah, in their mind eighteen centuries after God revealed the Torah to Moses at Mount Sinai, the Bavli's authorship remade the two received systems,

---

by-point consultation with Leviticus 16. But there are numerous other examples of a mere paraphrase, by Mishnah's authorship, of passages of Scripture (along with many more in which Scripture has nothing to say on topics dealt with in the Mishnah, or in which what Scripture thinks important about a topic is simply ignored as of no interest in the Mishnah).

the Pentateuchal and the Mishnaic. In its own rhetoric, in accord with its own topical program, appealing to a logic unique to itself among all Jewish minds in ancient times, that authorship presented the Torah of Sinai precisely as it wished to represent it. And it did so defiantly, not discretely and by indirection. Not merely alleging that Moses had written it all down, like the Pentateuchal compilers, nor modestly identifying with the direction of the Holy Spirit the choices that it made, like the Christians responsible for making the Bible, nor even, as with the framers of the Mishnah, sedulously sides-tepping, in laconic and disingenuous innocence, the issue of authority and tradition entirely. Quite the opposite, the Bavli's intellectuals took over the entire tradition, scriptural and mishnaic alike, chose what they wanted, tacked on to the selected passages their own words in their own way, and then put it all out as a single statement of their own.

True, they claimed for their system the standing of mere amplification of that tradition. But, as a matter of fact, they did say it all in their own words and they did set forth the whole of their statement in their own way, and – as above all – without recapitulating the received choices of ignoring or merely absorbing the received revelation, they represented as the one whole Torah revealed by God to Moses, our rabbi, at Sinai what they themselves had made up, and they made it stick. And that, I think, is the supreme hubris of the Jewish mind from the beginnings, in the Pentateuch, to the conclusion and climax in the Bavli. I like to think that that hubris of theirs at least for the beauty of it explains the success of what they made up,[25] on the simple principle, the more daring, the more plausible. For theirs was the final realization and statement in the formation of the Jewish intellect. Their mode of making connections and drawing conclusions defined, from then to now, the systems and the traditions of Judaisms.

---

[25]But of course the reason for the Bavli's enormous authority throughout the world of Judaism from Islamic times to ours cannot in the end be merely aesthetic. That is an issue to be worked out in its own terms.

Index

Amos 40

Aristotle 51, 53-55, 57, 67, 71, 74, 82-84

Avot 31, 116, 117

Babylonia 2-4, 19, 39-41, 43, 113, 114

Baron, Salo W. 61-64

Bauer, Walter 121

Bavli 4, 19, 20, 25, 31, 44, 113-122, 125, 127, 128

Bible 3, 22, 32, 35, 113-115, 120-128

Brooks, Roger 56

canon 5, 10, 12, 13, 22, 25-27, 29, 30, 42, 97, 100, 111, 114, 116, 117, 120-126

canonical writings 11, 12, 26, 27, 29, 30, 35, 36, 97, 126

Childs, Brevard S. 122, 123, 125

Christian 5, 15, 22, 31, 33, 66, 68, 89, 90, 92, 98, 99, 101, 102, 104, 109-115, 120-127

Christianity 3, 5, 31, 35, 51, 53, 66, 67, 89-91, 93, 97, 99-102, 104, 105, 108-115, 120-127

church 91, 92, 99, 109, 110, 113, 114, 120-125

context 5, 10-12, 14, 15, 17, 20, 21, 25, 26, 28-34, 37, 46, 47, 56, 59, 66-68, 72, 77, 79, 82, 90, 94, 95, 97, 102, 104, 108, 114, 125

Cyrus 2

Deuteronomy 4, 37, 38, 43, 45, 96, 119

dual Torah 2-5, 10-12, 30-32, 35, 55, 56, 66, 69, 84, 102, 113, 114, 118, 120, 122, 124

economic 21, 51, 52, 55-68, 70-72, 82, 85, 103

economics 9, 21, 22, 32, 33, 51-61, 64, 66-72, 74, 79, 82-84, 103

Essene 22, 35, 104, 126

Exodus 4, 37, 43, 45

Ezekiel 35, 36

Ezra 40, 116, 117

Finley, Moses I. 22

Flesher, Paul V. 22

Fox-Genovese, Elizabeth 55

Genesis 3, 4, 31, 32, 37, 38, 43, 102, 114, 119

Genesis Rabbah 4, 31, 32, 102, 114, 119

Gottfried, Paul E. 72

Harnack, Adolf 123

Humphreys, Sally C. 84

Humphreys, W. Lee 44

Isaiah 36

Islam 5, 10, 51-53, 67, 68, 104

Israel 1-5, 12, 14, 28, 30, 32, 35-48, 52, 53, 56, 66, 68, 69, 84,